HOW TO READ BUILDINGS

HOW TO READ BUILDINGS

A crash course in architectural styles

RIZZOLI
NEW YORK

Carol Davidson Cragoe

First published in the United States of America in
2008 by Rizzoli International Publications, Inc.
300 Park Avenue South
New York, NY 10010
www.rizzoliusa.com

This book was created by
IVY PRESS
The Old Candlemakers
Lewes, East Sussex BN7 2NZ, UK

2008 2009 2010 2011 / 10 9 8 7 6 5 4 3 2 1

ISBN: 978-0-8478-3112-8

Library of Congress Control Number:
2007931977

CREATIVE DIRECTOR Peter Bridgewater
PUBLISHER Jason Hook
EDITORIAL DIRECTOR Caroline Earle
ART DIRECTOR Sarah Howerd
SENIOR PROJECT EDITOR Dominique Page
DESIGN JC Lanaway
ILLUSTRATOR James Neal

Printed in China

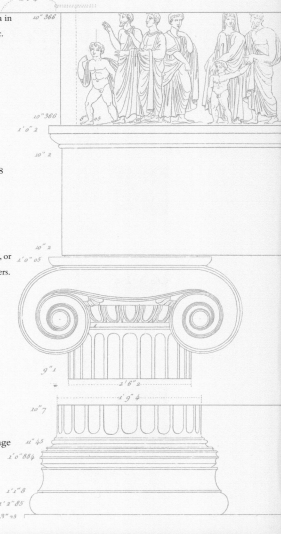

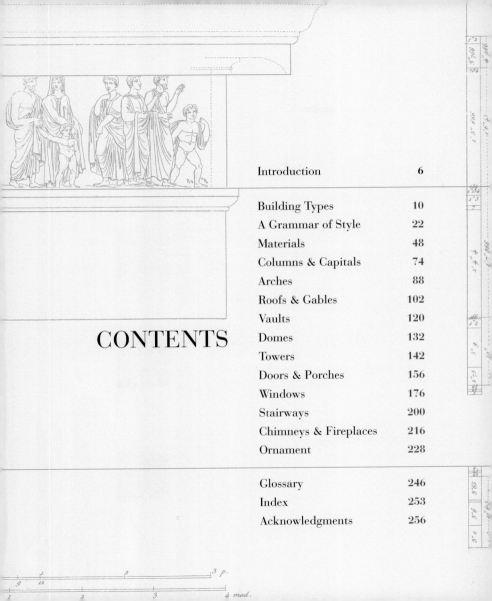

CONTENTS

Most of us pass hundreds of buildings every day, and it is easy enough to see that some of them are different or special. But how are they different? When were they built, and why? This book will help you find the answers to these questions and give you the skills you need to understand buildings. Using detailed engravings of whole buildings and individual parts, you will learn to recognize the key characteristics of structures dating from every period from the ancient Greeks right through to the present day.

Architecture—the art of building—has a language of its own, and reading buildings is just like reading in any language: you need to understand the basic components before you start, but once you are confident with the structure of the language, you can read anything.

Three key aspects make up the grammar of architectural language: period-based styles, different building types, and structural materials; all of these greatly influence the way a building looks, so each has been given a section in this book. Within this "grammatical" structure, there is an architectural vocabulary of individual building parts, including elements such as columns, fireplaces, roofs, stairs, windows, and doors. Decorative ornament is also an important part of this vocabulary. Again, each has its own section in this book, but as you will discover, the grammatical structure of style, building type, and materials provides a coherent framework into which each individual part fits.

RIGHT *The Temple of Hephaestus, Athens, built c.449 BCE using the Doric Order; it was converted into a Christian church in the 7th century.*

Reading a building

Before we start on the specifics, let's take a look at one example showing how the architectural language fits together. Consider the two buildings that are shown here. Don't get too hung up on what or where they are; simply notice what is similar about them and what is different. The differences are obvious: the Temple of Hephaestus on the left is long and low, while St. Pancras Church on the right has a tall tower in the middle. Look a bit more closely and some similarities begin to emerge: in particular, the row of six columns topped by a triangular pediment on the front of the church looks very like the front of the temple, although the detailing on the church is lighter and more delicate. This isn't a coincidence. The church, built in the early 19th century, is in the Greek Revival style, so its detailing deliberately imitates that of an ancient Greek temple. Once you have read this book, you will find comparisons such as this easy to make.

RIGHT *St. Pancras Church, London, built in 1819–22 in the Greek Revival style; it has an Ionic portico and a Classically inspired steeple.*

Looking for Clues

Understanding buildings is like detective work: you need to look for clues that will lead you to recognize the building. These clues might be windows that have been altered, changes in materials, or fragments of older structures left behind during alteration work, or they might be smaller, subtle things such as minor details or curious irregularities that make you wonder why the building is like that. Every structure is different, and like a good detective you need to approach each one with an open mind. However, there are some common clues that you can look out for.

The impact of details

As these pictures demonstrate, it is extremely important to look both at details and at the underlying form when trying to understand a building. These three houses are exactly the same inside, but use different exterior details, such as vertical pilasters or horizontal string courses, making them seem dissimilar.

Roof scars

Most alterations to a building leave some sort of mark or trace on the fabric. Here the roofline has been changed to make it flatter, leaving the edge of the former roof exposed (1). The projecting stub of a former wall (2) is also a clue to a now-lost structure.

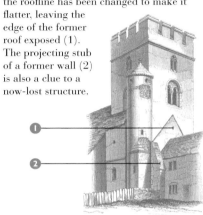

Altered windows

Being able to recognize aspects from different styles can be helpful in understanding just how a building developed. Here, a large 15th-century window, recognizable by its tracery, has been inserted in place of two 12th-century openings, which are still partly visible. This helps to reveal how this church changed over time.

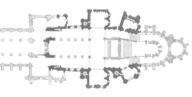

Oddities

Unusual or irregular features are often a good clue to changes that have been made to a building. At Canterbury Cathedral in England, for instance, the in-and-out curve at the east end (here on right) reveals an earlier structure that was only partially demolished when the new east end of the cathedral was built in the 1170s to 1180s.

Inserted floor

This Italian civic building must have had a floor inserted in the 18th century, because the store fronts with neoclassical windows above are at odds with the surrounding medieval arches, which would originally have been open. The external staircase is also a clue to this altered internal arrangement.

Introduction

The function of a building can influence its appearance, and many types of buildings have distinctive features that make them easy to recognize, such as a church tower or a store window. Often these features have a practical as well as a decorative purpose: a church tower, for instance, may hold the bells used to call people to worship. Familiarity with these key features will help you recognize different sorts of buildings, but elements from one type of building can also be used as decorative items on an entirely different sort of building, often to try and link one type of construction with another.

Church spire

Many building types have particular features that distinguish them from others, such as the minaret of a mosque, the large doorways of a warehouse, or the oversized windows that characterize stores. The spire of St. Pancras Church in London, built in 1819–22, clearly marks it out as a church, although it has a decorative temple front.

Temple facade

The distinctive front of a Classical temple, with its prominent pediment supported on columns, helps to conceal the *cella*, or sanctuary building, within, as here in the Temple of Dionysus, Teos, Turkey. The temple front was widely used as a decorative form in the Renaissance, baroque, and neoclassical periods.

Combined features

It is helpful to be able to recognize the characteristics of many different building types, because some buildings combine more than one form. The Knights' Hall of Malbork Castle, Poland, for instance, uses a fortified tower form, but adds to it the large, decorative windows that are characteristic of an aristocratic residence.

Railway station

New functions have required new building types to be developed, such as railway stations. King's Cross in London, built in 1851–2, was one of the earliest stations and clearly shows the large, arched train sheds on the building's exterior. It also has a prominent clock and a large waiting area.

Colonnaded terrace

The early 19th-century Park Terrace in London, designed by John Nash, is actually a long row of houses attached to each other on either side, but the projecting colonnade serves to unify the entire design and create a whole that is grander than any individual house on its own.

Religious

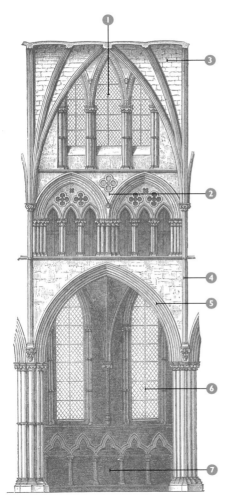

The form of a sacred building varies from one religion to another, but most share the characteristic of providing a space in which worshippers can gather. In many religions this space is subdivided according to gender, and there may also be special areas for those who are not yet fully initiated into the religion. Religions that include a ritual carried out by priests, such as the Christian mass, usually also have a place reserved for this purpose, which may or may not be visible to the faithful. Religious buildings are often among the most prominent in a locality and may be further distinguished by domes or tall towers that punctuate the skyline.

Church elevation

Large medieval churches are multistory buildings, and the arrangement of parts vertically is known as the elevation. Key parts of the elevation of a church or cathedral include the high-level clerestory windows (1), triforium (2), vaults (3), vault responds (4), nave arcades (5), aisle windows (6), and blind arcading (7), though not all churches have all of these elements.

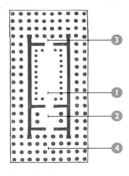

Temple plan

The interior *cella* (1) of a Greek temple held a statue of the deity commemorated. It had no windows and was reserved for the priests, while worshippers stood outside. In front was the *pronaos* (2), behind was the *epinaos* (3), and the whole was usually surrounded by a colonnade or peristyle (4).

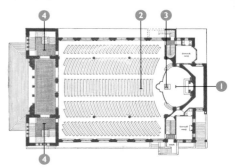

Synagogue

A synagogue is a Jewish religious building, and includes a raised platform at the east end (1) for the Ark holding the holy scrolls, a large area (2) for seating, and a reading desk or *bema* (3). Here at Temple Beth-el, New York (1892), there are also women's galleries accessed by stairs (4).

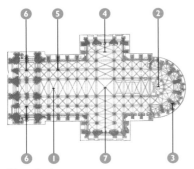

Church plan

A Christian church has two main parts: the nave (1) where worshippers gather, and the choir (2) where the mass is celebrated. Larger churches, like Cologne Cathedral, Germany, seen here, are more complex, and often include a curving apse (3), transepts (4), aisles (5), and western towers (6), as well as a central crossing (7).

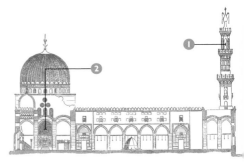

Mosque

Islamic places of worship are called mosques. Key features include a tall tower, named a minaret (1), for calling the faithful to prayer, and a large hall (2), usually domed, where worshippers gather for their prayers and to hear sermons. Seen here is the 12th-century Sultan Barkuk mosque in Cairo, Egypt (*c.*1149).

Castle & Palace

A castle is a defensible fortification, and a palace is a grand royal or aristocratic residence, but the distinction between the two was often blurred in the Middle Ages, with castles having luxurious living accommodation and palaces having strong outer defenses. Towers were also an important part of medieval fortifications and aristocratic residences. From the 17th century onwards, fortification and aristocratic accommodation were increasingly separated, and palace architecture developed as a showcase for the owner's wealth and prestige. Many great houses were built in the 18th and 19th centuries, and other new forms of buildings—notably the grand hotel—also borrowed the vocabulary of palace architecture.

Medieval castle

The medieval castle of the Old Louvre in Paris (whose remains can be seen under the present Louvre) was strongly fortified, with a gatehouse (1), corner turrets (2), and a central keep tower (3), but it also had luxurious lodgings (4) and a chapel (5) for the king and his family.

Renaissance palace

The *palazzo*, or palace, of the Medici family in Florence (begun 1444) is a typical Italian Renaissance palace, with a strong-walled lower floor providing space for storage of goods and an entrance onto the central courtyard. The main living accommodation was on the upper floors, which have large biforate windows.

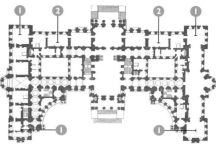

Turreted palace

Blenheim Palace, England, was built for the Duke of Marlborough in 1705–22. Its corner turrets (1) hint at fortification and the military victories the palace commemorates, but they are decorative, not functional. As was common in this period, the luxurious main rooms are *enfilade*—linked to one another without a separate corridor (2).

Millionaire's mansion

The hugely wealthy trade and industry magnates of the 19th century built themselves enormous houses that are palaces in all but name. One such is the Vanderbilt family's Italianate house, The Breakers, in Newport, Rhode Island, which has 78 rooms. Designed by Richard Morris Hunt, it was built in 1893–95.

Grand hotel

Hotels, which became an increasingly important building type as the development of trains and steamships during the 19th century promoted mass travel, borrowed the visual language of palaces to create very grand buildings. Raffles Hotel in Singapore (1887), for instance, combines Palladian windows with locally derived motifs.

Domestic

Houses are the main type of building that surrounds us, but house design has changed considerably over the centuries. In the ancient world—and still in many hot countries today—houses were built around a central courtyard with rooms opening off the sides. In medieval Europe, the key element of houses was the great hall, a large open room that served as kitchen, eating place, and sleeping area. In the 16th century, compartmentalized private spaces, including those on upper floors, became more common. The growth of cities also led to the development of terraces, or rows of houses linked at the sides.

Tuscan atrium
The interior of this *atrium tuscanum* (Tuscan atrium) shows the extremely rich internal finishes of ancient Roman houses. The central atrium, which is open to the sky, has a coffered ceiling and painted frescoes on the walls. Individual rooms opened onto it, and there was a central water feature.

Great hall

The great hall was the main living area in a medieval house, serving as both a communal eating and sleeping space, and was typically open to the roof, with large windows. The two doors at the far end provided access to the pantry and buttery for dry and wet food storage respectively.

Jettied urban house

Even without going inside, it is possible to tell that this medieval French house has several stories. The projecting jetties, which represent the ends of floor joists cantilevered out for strength, clearly indicate the presence of floors. The jetty beam along the front of the house is often heavily decorated.

Suburban house

How can we be certain that this is a house, and not a store, for instance? Partly, because of its size, not too large nor too small, but also because of the single entrance and the windows, which are much the same size on all floors—unlike store windows, which would be larger at ground level.

Apartment block

The Highpoint apartments in London's Highgate were built c.1935, and you can clearly recognize them as apartments by the prominent single entrance and multiple windows over many stories. The blocks were designed in such a way as to provide each apartment with good light and air.

Public

Most societies have some sort of public buildings for civic and governmental purposes, for large-scale entertainments, and for housing collections that are open to many people. Among the most common types of public buildings are theaters, governmental buildings, libraries, and museums. Such buildings have architectural vocabularies of their own, which are distinguishable from those of religious, domestic, or commercial buildings; and certain key features—such as the prominent towers of town and city halls—are widely seen. Public buildings also have distinctive internal arrangements, such as the auditorium of a theater or the open gallery spaces of a museum.

Theater
This cutaway view of an ancient Greek theater shows how similar it was to a modern theater. Seating was raked or angled back to give everyone a good view; the action took place on a raised stage above the orchestra, for musicians and dancers; and behind were dressing rooms and storage areas.

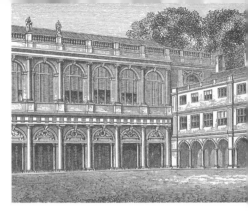

Town hall

The 15th-century late Gothic town hall in Brussels, Belgium, has a very prominent tower, which had a clock and also housed bells. Not only did the tower make the clock more visible above the city, but it was also a prominent marker of civic pride and local power.

College library

A library has always been fundamental to schools, colleges, and universities. The 17th-century library of Trinity College, Cambridge, England, has large windows supplying good natural light in the upper-floor reading room. The lower arcades conceal the area with the book stacks.

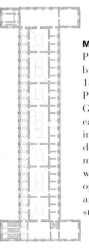

Museum

Public museums were a new building form in the late 18th century, and the Alte Pinakothek in Munich, Germany, was one of the earliest. It has a series of interconnected galleries down the middle of the museum, lit from above, with smaller galleries opening off at the sides, an arrangement that is still common in museums.

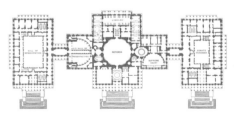

Government building

The architectural form of the US Capitol building reflects the structure of the US government with its two elected bodies, the Senate and the House of Representatives. Each has a large chamber, one at either end, and in the center is a domed entrance rotunda. There is a smaller court chamber.

Commercial

Every society that buys, sells, or makes things needs places where these goods can be produced and stored, as well as places where buyers and sellers can meet. A commercial space can be as simple as a blanket spread on the ground, but as cities developed it became desirable to have buildings dedicated to such purposes where goods could be both stored and sold. In cities, the pressure on space meant that urban stores were often combined with residential premises, either for the owner to live in or to let out. In the 19th century the department store selling all types of goods was developed.

Stoa

The ancient Greek *stoa*, a type of one- or two-storied covered colonnade, was an early shopping center and often surrounded a marketplace. Small stores were constructed against the solid wall at the back, while the open colonnade at the front provided a shady walkway for shoppers and other pedestrians.

Commercial and domestic

The pressure on space in cities meant that stores and dwellings were, and still are, often combined in the same building. This late medieval French building had a store on the ground floor and several levels of dwellings above, which may have been used by different families, much like modern apartments.

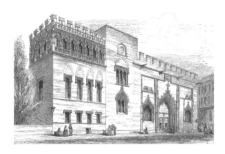

Market house

The increasing amount of international trade during the Middle Ages led to the development of buildings for merchants in trading centers such as port cities. This late medieval Spanish *casa lonja* (commerce or market house) in Valencia has thick walls and heavily barred windows to protect the goods being stored there.

Department store

Department stores like Bloomingdale's in New York were invented in the 19th century and brought together a wide variety of different goods previously sold in separate stores. You can easily recognize them by their very prominent entrances, inviting customers in, and by their large display windows at street level.

Warehouse

The late 19th-century Dalton Brothers' warehouse and showrooms in Sydney, Australia, features large openings for carts and prominent ground-floor windows. Such buildings were not only practical places to keep goods and transact business, but, in using the latest architectural fashions, served as large advertisements for their owners.

Introduction

Style is what helps us recognize when a building was built and sometimes also what it was for, and we will look at some of the key styles here. Architectural styles have changed considerably over time, and as with other fashions, older styles are sometimes revived. Architectural style has two key components: individual decorative details, and the overall arrangement of all the parts of the building. Thus, both a Greek temple and a Gothic cathedral use pointed gables, but the temple is easily distinguished from the cathedral by the appearance and placement of the gables and by other details, such as the use of tracery and buttresses on the cathedral.

Reuse of motifs

Most architectural styles contain elements of older styles as well as new motifs. The Renaissance style, seen here in the Scuola Grande di San Marco, Venice (c.1480s–90s), used many Roman-derived motifs, such as the arch set beneath an entablature on columns, pediments, and coffering, but combined them in new ways.

Temple style and construction

The key stylistic characteristics of Greek temples, the pediment and the portico of columns, both had structural as well as decorative functions. As shown here, the columns supported a ceiling over an open walkway around the building, while the pediment unified and concealed the roofs over both the central *cella* building and the outer portico.

Gothic window

All the main elements of the Gothic style are present in this 14th-century window from Chartres Cathedral in France: pointed arches, decorative gables, window tracery (shaped stone bars), and niches with statues. Being able to recognize this kind of detail helps you identify when a building was built and what it was for.

Roman arcade

Arches set underneath a lintel supported by columns, seen here on the 1st-century BCE Theater of Marcellus in Rome, are a key stylistic feature of Roman architecture. This style originated in the use of arches to strengthen the relatively weak trabeated (post-and-lintel) construction used by the Greeks.

Neoclassical detail

Architectural style can be used to evoke particular historical periods and also to symbolize certain characteristics, such as wealth or class. The designer of this early 20th-century American suburban house used neoclassical style details to evoke the grandeur of the pre–Civil War American South.

Greek

Ancient Greek architecture was fundamentally a representation of timber-post-and-beam, or trabeated, construction in stone, and most surviving buildings are temples. Rows of tall columns supported a lintel, which in turn supported a pitched roof structure running the length of the building. The triangular gable formed at either end of the pitched roof was often heavily decorated and was a key feature of the style. Strict rules, known as the Orders, governed the design of each part of the building, including the size and shape of the columns, the ornament on the capitals, and the design of the entablature area above the capitals.

Early Corinthian Order

One of the earliest examples of the ornate Corinthian Order was the Choragic Monument of Lysicrates (335–334 BCE), located at the foot of the Acropolis in Athens. It was intended to carry a bronze bowl won in a choral competition by Lysicrates as a thank-you offering to the gods.

Doric Order

The Doric Order, with relatively simple capitals, fluted columns, and alternating grooved triglyphs and plain or sculpted metopes, was particularly characteristic of mainland Greek architecture. Unlike the later Roman Doric, Greek Doric columns have no bases. The columns swell slightly in the middle to make them appear more graceful.

Temple plan

The design of Greek temples was based on strict rules of proportion governing all parts, and usually included an outer peristyle (colonnade) around the inner sanctuary, which was composed of the *pronaos* entrance porch, the main *cella* or *naos* room, and the *opisthodomos* behind.

Cella

The *cella* at the heart of a Greek temple was reserved for the priests. Here was the statue of the god or goddess, with the offerings brought by the people. The *cella* was enclosed by the colonnaded portico, and the altar was usually placed on the top step, or stylobate.

Painted decoration

Today we think of Greek architecture as being characterized by the use of plain white marble, but originally it would have been brightly painted in gaudy colors. This illustration shows how a seemingly unornamented and plain Doric capital and column might have been painted with geometric and leaf patterns.

Roman

The Romans made a number of important technological discoveries, including the structural possibilities of the arch, the use of concrete, and the development of the dome. These innovations enabled the construction of much larger and more complex buildings than had been possible with the simpler Greek trabeated construction system. The use of arches also increased the Romans' range of decorative possibilities, most notably arches within a system of columns and entablature. Surface decoration, on both walls and ceilings, also became much richer. Later, the lavishness of Roman architecture was seen by critics to symbolize both the decadence and decline of the Empire.

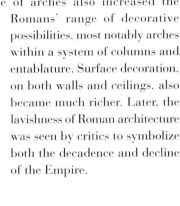

Roman elaboration
Roman architecture, especially temple architecture (as here in the 1st-century BCE Temple of Fortuna Virilis), shared many basic characteristics with Greek architecture, including the prominent portico, use of the Orders (here Ionic), and the stepped podium. However, it tended to be more ornate and elaborate overall.

Structural arch

The motif of an arch within an entablature frame, as here on the Colosseum in Rome, was a key Roman feature. It arose from a reluctance to abandon the appearance of trabeated construction with columns supporting a lintel, even if the weight was really being borne by the arches.

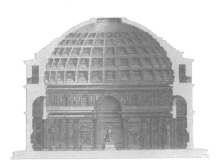

Concrete dome

The characteristic hemispherical dome and rich interior decoration of the Pantheon, Rome (c.118–28 CE), were hugely influential on later architecture. The Pantheon was a temple dedicated to all the gods, and its enormous concrete dome was not surpassed until the Renaissance. It was converted into a church in the early 7th century.

Late Roman palace complex

The late Roman emperor Diocletian built a vast palace and temple complex at Split in Croatia (c.300–306 CE). The entrance courtyard, seen here with later buildings inserted into it, has an arcade with Corinthian columns. Notice the heavy cornice above, and observe how the arches are now freed from an outer frame.

Roman domestic building

The discovery in the late 18th century of the lost city of Pompeii, near Naples, was particularly significant for the development of neoclassical architecture because it revealed Roman domestic buildings such as houses, basilicas, and baths in a far more perfect state of preservation than had been seen previously.

Early Christian & Byzantine

Christianity became the official religion of the Roman Empire in 326 CE following the conversion a few years earlier of the Emperor Constantine. Roman architectural forms were adapted to new Christian uses, and in particular the aisled basilica, used by the Romans as an assembly hall, became the common model for Christian churches. Architectural ornament was also adapted to the new religion. Roman building traditions were largely abandoned in Europe after the fall of the Empire in the 5th century, but persisted in the eastern part known as Byzantium and in its capital, Constantinople, today called Istanbul, Turkey.

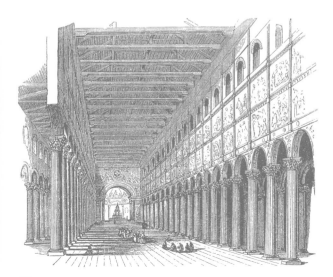

Aisled basilica
A typical five-aisled basilica plan had a high central nave lit by a clerestory and lower side aisles, as at S. Paolo fuori le Mura in Rome, built during Constantine's reign. The apse, which was used in Roman basilicas for tribunals, held the altar, while the congregation assembled in the nave.

Domed basilica

The basilica was further adapted through the introduction of a central dome, which provided more light in the middle of the building. The Hagia Sophia, Constantinople (Istanbul), 532–37 CE, was one of the most important domed basilicas. As well as the main dome, it had subdomes, creating a cruciform, or cross-shaped, plan.

Outer narthex

The narthex, or porch, was an important part of early Christian churches. Unbaptized believers could not attend the mass itself, so they withdrew to the narthex during the second part of the service. The narthex at Old St. Peter's, Rome, had a further open-air atrium, or courtyard, for large gatherings.

Mosaic decoration

The interiors of early Christian and Byzantine churches, such as that of S. Constanza, Rome, were often lavishly decorated with mosaics—pictures made up of tiny squares of colored glass and stone. Gold-backed tiles were also used, especially for backgrounds, giving a shimmering, unworldly effect.

Christian capital

Byzantine capitals were adapted from Corinthian capitals, but were simplified and stylized. In this example from St. Mark's, Venice, stylized, but still recognizable, acanthus leaves curl around a central Christian cross, but birds, beasts, and foliage stylized to the point of becoming purely geometric were also common.

Romanesque

Romanesque architecture is characterized by the use of round arches, thick walls, and heavy, geometric decoration. The Romanesque style developed around the year 1000 CE and was widespread across Europe until the late 12th century, when it was supplanted by the new Gothic style. Its name highlights its derivation from ancient Roman buildings, but Romanesque is also known as Norman in England and France, because it was brought to England by the Normans after the Conquest of 1066. Many of the finest surviving Romanesque buildings are found along the pilgrimage route to the cathedral of Santiago de Compostela in northern Spain.

Apsidal chapel
The small apsidal chapels that reflect the curve of the main apse, and are echoed in the round tower, provide the exterior of St. Sernin in Toulouse, France (1080–90), with visual strength through the massing of relatively simple forms. The layers of round-headed windows and blind arcading repeat the theme and provide horizontal definition.

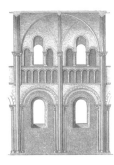

Romanesque elevation

A typical Romanesque elevation has the round arches of the nave arcades carried on clustered piers, as in the church of Holy Trinity, Caen, France. A central shaft provides vertical definition into bays, while the blind arcading of the small triforium gives horizontal definition. The clerestory windows are flanked by blind niches.

Ornamental variety

Variety, especially variety in ornament, is one of the hallmarks of the Romanesque style. In the cloister of S. Paolo, Rome, for instance, each set of paired shafts is different from its neighbors, and there is even variety within some of the pairs of columns. The capitals are also varied.

Blind arcading

Romanesque ornament is generally strong, not subtle, and usually includes geometric motifs and grotesque animal or human forms. A contemporary described the Romanesque decoration at Canterbury Cathedral, like this blind arcading of c.1120, as having been "carved with an ax not a chisel."

Romanesque door

The doors into Romanesque buildings were particularly heavily decorated, which served to emphasize the transition from the secular world outside to the sacred world inside. The decoration was intended to inspire awe and religious fervor in the viewer with, as here, images of Christ in Judgment and scenes of saints and sinners.

Gothic

The development of the pointed arch in the 12th century opened up a huge range of new architectural possibilities, leading to the development of the Gothic style. Notice how Gothic buildings are much higher and lighter than their Romanesque predecessors and have much larger windows. Tracery, the stone latticework inside a window, developed during this period, and rib vaults became standard. As masons became increasingly confident during the later Middle Ages, new, more complex forms developed. In particular, the use of the ogee or S-shaped arch enabled the development of flowing tracery and decorative patterns and the construction of shallower, less steeply pointed arches.

French early Gothic

Typical of French early Gothic architecture of the 12th century are the three west doors, or portals, surmounted by three pointed lancets and a rose window, and flanked by tall towers with spires, on the west facade of Chartres Cathedral, France. The rib vaults inside are revealed by the flying buttresses outside.

Elegant ambulatory

Gothic masons were capable of creating very delicate effects, rather like fine metalwork, as evidenced by the early 13th-century ambulatory at Auxerre Cathedral in France. Although the walls are actually very solid, their weight is disguised by freestanding elongated shafts, many large windows, and blind arcading.

English Perpendicular

The use of tall mullions and horizontal transoms to create a paneled effect in the lower part of the window is characteristic of the English late Gothic variant called Perpendicular. This 15th-century window in Hull, England, uses both pointed and ogee arches to create a complex, intersecting tracery pattern.

Decorated style

English Gothic architecture of the 14th century is often called the Decorated style because of its rich surface treatments. Here, in the early 14th-century chapter house at Wells Cathedral, England, the central shaft is composed of many small shafts, the ribs have multiplied, and the tracery patterns are very complex.

Gothic market cross

Gothic styling was not restricted to churches. Here, Gothic detailing is applied to the very secular form of a market cross in Chichester, England (c.1500). Such structures provided a central focus for the market as well as a shelter below. The Chichester cross also has a clock, which was a 14th-century invention.

Renaissance

Italian architects rejected the elaboration of the Gothic during the 15th century, using a Classically inspired style that reintroduced the Orders and incorporated pediments, strong horizontal entablatures, flat ceilings, and other Roman motifs. The Renaissance style spread throughout Europe in the 16th and early 17th centuries. Outside Italy, architects felt freer to ignore the strict rules that had originally governed the Orders and developed their own variations, using Classical motifs to create new styles, and new forms such as shaped gables and strapwork appeared in northern Europe. *All'antica* motifs based on ancient designs were also popular, and included obelisks, urns, trailing foliage, and playful *putti*.

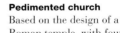

Pedimented church
Based on the design of a Roman temple, with four giant pilasters supporting a pediment, the facade of S. Andrea, Mantua, Italy, was begun in 1470. The design was adapted for use as a church by means of Christian sculpture over the main entrance and by the presence of doors into the side aisles.

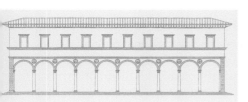

Arcade and entablature

Early Italian Renaissance architecture had a stark simplicity, as embodied in the 1490s arcade of Piazza S. Maria Novella in Florence. The simple round arches of the arcade are carried on Corinthian columns, with only roundels as decoration. There are no other verticals, only the strong horizontals of the entablature and windows above.

Symmetrical facade

The Renaissance placed a new emphasis on symmetry. In his 1580s design for Wollaton Hall in Nottingham, England, Robert Smythson created a perfectly symmetrical entrance facade, hiding the nature of the rooms behind evenly spaced windows. This contrasts with medieval buildings, where spaces were expressed on the outside.

Northern Renaissance

Northern European Renaissance architects felt free to combine different motifs to create a decorative effect. The elaborately shaped gable of Leiden Town Hall in the Netherlands (1596) is topped by a series of obelisks, with pediments breaking the horizontal line of the parapet, and different types of columns and pilasters freely mixed.

All'antica motifs

Decorative designs based on antique motifs such as urns, grotesque figures, foliage, shells, vases, and cartouches were hugely popular in the Renaissance. Designs for these motifs were circulated as prints, something made much simpler and cheaper after the development of the printing press in the late 15th century.

Baroque & Rococo

The baroque style developed in the early 17th century, and was characterized by a grand elaboration of detail and space. Architects took Classical motifs and recombined them to create a sense of drama. The Giant Order was characteristic, and new motifs like the broken pediment appeared. The baroque is particularly associated with the great Roman Catholic churches of the Counter-Reformation and with European palace architecture. Rococo is a softer, less formal version that developed in early 18th-century Paris. Most commonly associated with interior decoration, it was characterized by light, playful ornament using scallop shells, C-curves, and scrolls.

Curving facade

Francesco Borromini was one of the most important baroque architects. His church of S. Carlo alle Quattro Fontane, in Rome (1665–67), uses alternating convex and concave surfaces to articulate the facade, which projects forward in the center. The curving motif is further articulated by the oval cartouche and by the broken ogee pediment.

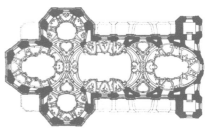

Monumental motifs

Key baroque motifs include giant Orders of pilasters to unify stories, broken pediments, and exaggerated keystones above the windows. All of these motifs can be seen in the design of Greenwich Hospital, London (*c.*1695). The wall surfaces are further elaborated with rustication. The overall effect is grand and monumental, yet varied.

Curved plan forms

The use of rounded shapes was not only limited to elevations. Baroque and rococo architects also exploited curves for plan forms, such as the intersecting ovals and circles used by J. B. Neumann for the church of Vierzehnheiligen, in Germany (1742–72). These shapes were repeated in curving vaults.

Rococo ornament

C-shaped curves were typical of rococo ornament, and were often used in combination with scrolls, shells, and swags. Ornament was not limited to architectural elements such as windows and doors, but spread over walls, ceilings, and other surfaces. This French paneling is representative of a widely used type.

Curved pediment

Both curved and broken pediments are characteristic baroque motifs, where architects took a Classical form and expanded its decorative possibilities. This Parisian example has a curved broken-based pediment on consoles with floral moldings; it is further enriched with a central female bust set amid floral swags.

Palladian

The 16th-century Italian architect Andrea Palladio (1508–1580) had a huge impact on later architecture, especially in the 18th and early 19th centuries. His buildings are characterized by the use of a pedimented temple front, symmetrical planning, and the so-called Palladian or Serlian window. Palladio's work was brought to a wider audience through books of his designs. The first English Palladian architect was Inigo Jones (1573–1652), but it was the amateur architect Lord Burlington who made the style fashionable in the early 18th century. Palladianism was common in England and the United States.

Porticoed church
A typical Palladian arrangement has a central structure with a porticoed temple front flanked by two smaller pavilions, as at Inigo Jones's St. Paul's in Covent Garden, London (1631). Jones's work was not immediately influential because of the English Civil War, but Palladianism returned to England in the early 18th century.

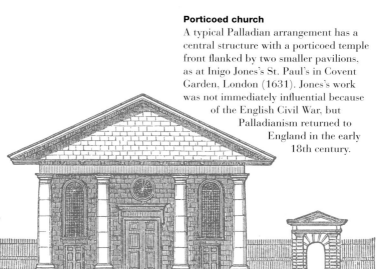

Temple facade atop a podium

Raised up on a podium, a classic example of Palladianism, Lord Burlington's Chiswick House, London (begun 1725), was one of the most influential Palladian buildings. The front (seen here) has a temple facade and a half-round Diocletian window in the dome. The complex stairs add drama and movement to the facade.

Coffered rotunda

The exterior of a pure Palladian building is clean-lined, with the emphasis placed on proportion and key details, but the interior decoration is in a richer Roman style. The central domed rotunda at Chiswick House, London, was coffered, with elaborate door, window, and picture surrounds to designs that were recommended by Palladio.

Dormer window

Palladianism was influential in colonial America. Here, for instance, a classic Palladian window with its central arched light breaking through an entablature above two lower flanking lights is used in a weatherboard-clad dormer window. The rusticated quoins and heavy cornice are also made in timber, not stone.

Temple-fronted rotunda

Another classic Palladian building is Thomas Jefferson's University of Virginia rotunda in Charlottesville. The central temple front has Corinthian columns, apses create a symmetrical oval plan, and the central rotunda is articulated by a dome, but the two stories of windows make it clear that this is a modern, building.

Neoclassical

The Enlightenment of the mid-18th century brought with it a new emphasis on the scientific study of the past, and people began to look more closely at the ruins of ancient Greece and Rome. Books of engravings taken directly from antique models were made more widely available, leading to a revival of Classical, especially Greek, styles, based very closely on antique models. Greek Revival neoclassical architecture was particularly popular in France and in the United States, where it was often called the Federal style, because its simplicity was seen as a suitably republican antidote to the decadence and overelaboration of imperial Roman architecture and its derivatives, like the baroque and rococo styles.

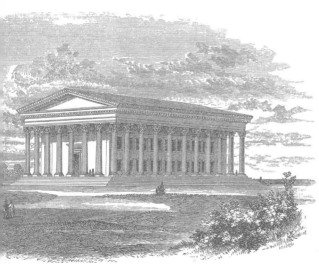

National style
Greek Revival was the pre-eminent style in early 19th-century America. Girard College school in Philadelphia (1833–48), designed by Thomas Walter, who also worked on the US Capitol, uses a temple form. A Corinthian portico completely encloses the *cella*-like inner building, which has windows, but the portico makes the interior dark.

Combination features

The Comédie-Française theater in Paris (1787–90) blended Greek, Roman, and Renaissance elements to create a simple, elegant building. It has a projecting portico without a pediment, a common feature of early neoclassical buildings. The facade and openings are rusticated, and there is also a Diocletian window above the portico.

Unifying portico

This long row, or terrace, of London houses, Park Crescent, designed by John Nash and built in 1812–22, uses an enormous columnar portico to unify the composition and create a single whole whose sum is much greater than its individual parts. From a distance, it looks like one palatial building.

Neoclassical fireplace

Motifs derived from ancient models were as important in interior as in exterior design. This fireplace features egg-and-dart banding, Greek key (or meander) pattern decoration, Classical draped female heads, garlands, and a central urn, probably derived from patterns available as engravings and from newly discovered remains.

Greek Revival house

The Greek Revival style was popular for houses because key details, such as the pediment and portico, could easily be added. This house has a Doric hexastyle (six-columned) portico at the front, and attached pilasters along the sides, but its sash windows clearly identify it as a 19th-century construction.

Gothic Revival

A revival of Gothic styles began in the late 18th century, initially only with the adoption of Gothic-style motifs such as tracery, but soon becoming full-scale copying of Gothic buildings, especially for churches. Gothic Revival houses were a prevalent style during 19th-century England. The Gothic Revival was part of a much larger movement that was known as the Picturesque, which also included landscape gardening. The Picturesque was characterized by irregularity and variety, creating a very dramatic appearance. Consequently, Gothic Revival architecture is also defined by deliberate irregularity, both to create a sense of the dramatic and to make the building look as if it developed naturally.

Sham Gothic
Made to look as if it might have been a medieval abbey, Fonthill Abbey house in Wiltshire, England was a key early Gothic Revival building, but its detailing was largely constructed of plaster and wood, not of the stone that was used during the Middle Ages. Unsurprisingly, its huge tower collapsed shortly after it was built.

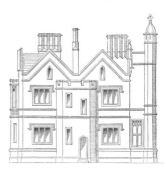

Gothic Revival house
The Gothic Revival style was very popular for houses such as this early 19th-century example. Key details that evoke the Gothic Revival style include pointed arches, crenellations, irregular chimneys, tracery windows, and a turret. Most of the detailing here is derived from the late Gothic period, but earlier Gothic details were also common.

National pride
In England, the Gothic Revival was an important statement of national pride, intended to evoke a period of religious and civic greatness in the late Middle Ages. Thus many important 19th-century English civic buildings, including the main Law Courts, seen here, and the Houses of Parliament in London, were Gothic Revival in style.

Gothic Revival church

Gothic Revival was a significant style for churches in the 19th century and became associated with attempts to revive the perceived religious fervor of the Middle Ages. Gothic Revival churches, such as Grace Church in New York, often copied medieval forms quite closely, but their scale and elaboration make them unmistakably later.

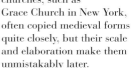

Urban adaptation
The church of All Saints, Margaret Street, London (1849–59), adapts Gothic Revival detailing to a difficult and cramped urban space. The tower is hugely tall to ensure that it can be seen high above other buildings, and the details are executed in brick and tile in order to withstand urban pollution and dirt.

Late 19th Century

The architecture of the late 19th century is often called Victorian after England's Queen Victoria (ruled 1837–1901). It is characterized by a variety of revival styles drawing on Classical, Romanesque, Gothic, and Renaissance motifs, as architects searched for ideas suitable for their era and for styles appropriate to different types of buildings. Among these were the Beaux-Arts style—a grandiose mix of Greek, Roman, Renaissance, and baroque motifs often used for large-scale public buildings—and the Queen Anne style, which was popular for smaller buildings like houses. Toward the end of the century wholly new styles such as Art Nouveau also began to emerge.

Beaux-Arts style

The Beaux-Arts style, named after the Ecole des Beaux-Arts in Paris, is characterized by an eclectic and very often grandiose combination of elements from the Greek, Roman, Renaissance, and baroque periods. The Paris Opera, opened in 1875, has a typically lavish mix of pediments, columns, domes, and statues.

Eclectic style

The Egyptian Halls in Glasgow, built in 1871–72, have a Renaissance-influenced iron facade with a heavy cornice, plus arcades on each level. The capitals and columns are eclectic, with Egyptian-style palmettes at the top, then Corinthian, then bracket capitals, and finally very plain, large display windows at ground level.

Queen Anne style

The Queen Anne style is characterized by asymmetry, small-paned windows, decorative gables, half-timbering, and fancy brick and tile work. It is seen here at Lowther House, London, designed by Richard Norman Shaw in 1875. Its American variations include the stick, shingle, and Eastlake styles.

Moorish style

The Great or Dohány Street Synagogue in Budapest, Hungary, built in 1854–59, is in a Moorish style inspired by Spanish and North African models, and has banded masonry, turrets with onion domes, and latticework windows. The Moorish style distinguished the synagogue from the Gothic Revival style that was then fashionable for churches.

Art Nouveau

Using curving forms often reminiscent of plant forms, Art Nouveau or "new art" broke away from a dependence on older models to create something wholly new. This sinuously curved staircase from the Hôtel Tassel in Brussels, Belgium, designed by Victor Horta in 1893–94, is an early example of the Art Nouveau style.

Modernism

In the 20th century, architects and designers experimented with ways of creating a new style of art and architecture that was specific to their era, rather than being based on a style of the past. After World War I, the Art Deco style was inspired by machines. It used geometric ornament and modern materials, including plastics and decorative metals like chrome. In the late 1920s International Modernism, which was plain and almost unornamented, began to emerge in the work of architects like Le Corbusier and the German Bauhaus school. After World War II Modernism was widely used for large-scale building projects, including offices and public housing.

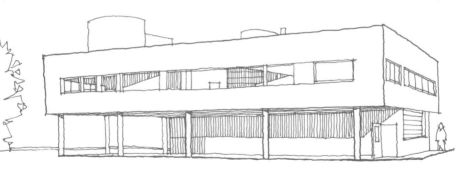

Modernist house
The Villa Savoye near Paris, designed by the architect Charles-Edouard Jeanneret (1887–1965), known as Le Corbusier, was an influential early Modernist building. Its clean lines without ornament, flat roof, large horizontal windowlike slits or ribbons, supporting columns, open-plan interior, and pure white exterior make it a "machine for living."

Art Deco style

The stylized geometric shapes and clean lines of the top of the Chrysler Building in New York (begun 1928) are characteristic of the Art Deco style, which was popular during the early 20th century. The arched forms are derived from Classical models, but are reinterpreted in new ways.

Modernist office

The Seagram Building in New York, which was completed in 1958 and designed by Ludwig Mies van der Rohe and Philip Johnson, is a classic example of Modernism. Entirely unadorned— with the exception of the structure, which is visible externally beneath the sheer glass walls—the building expresses its function as offices for large numbers of people.

Postmodernist detail

The oversized broken pediment that tops this office building is a typical Postmodernist detail. It makes reference to the past, but almost as a joke and not as an accurate copy of an earlier building. Other popular Postmodernist details include oversized columns, cornices and gables, and the use of bright colors.

Suburban house

The development of Modernist architecture for large-scale buildings had less of an impact at the level of the ordinary house. This 1940s house is in a style that originates in the Palladianism and neoclassicism of the 18th century.

MATERIALS Introduction

The actual materials that a building is made of greatly influence the way it looks. Materials also affect what can be built in the first place, and are a key determinant in defining different styles. For instance, a skyscraper could not be built without concrete foundations and a structural steel frame. This section looks at key building materials, such as stone, wood, glass, and steel, and explores how their use and development have influenced the course of architectural history. It also examines the decorative possibilities of the different materials, which can have a huge effect on the way we perceive a building.

Different detailing
The use of materials can make a huge difference to the way we perceive a building. For instance, this mid-17th-century house in Massachusetts has a jetty, like many European houses of the same date, but the horizontal wood siding makes it look very different from the exposed timber framing that was popular in Europe.

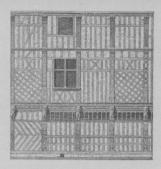

The advantages of stone

The great Gothic cathedrals (such as this one at Cologne), with their high vaults, flying buttresses, and huge stained-glass windows, were made possible by an increase in the understanding of the structural possibilities of stone. Gothic builders understood the key points that needed reinforcement to enable them to make very large openings.

Decorative structure

The intrinsic properties of certain materials can lead to characteristic decorative effects. You can see that the framing of this 16th-century French house in Beauvais is far more complex than is strictly necessary for structural stability, and exploits the decorative possibilities of patterns of dark timber against the light plaster infill.

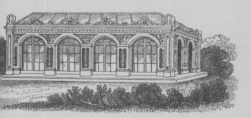

Spolia

Materials can be reused, either for economy or for symbolic purposes in an attempt to link a building with an earlier age. Salvaged materials, or *spolia*, from ancient Rome, like these Corinthian columns reused in a church, were particularly valued for their perceived connections with early Christianity and imperial glory.

Detached conservatory

The development of new manufacturing techniques, notably in the production of structural metals and glass, during the 18th and early 19th centuries enabled the construction of fully glazed structures like this English conservatory. Artificial heating would have been provided to allow tender plants to be grown all winter.

Stone

Stone is one of the oldest and most common walling materials, especially for religious and major civic buildings. Limestones and marbles of various kinds are the easiest to carve, but sandstone, granite, and lightweight volcanic stones such as tufa are also used. Mortar, a thin paste of lime or cement and water, is spread between the blocks to ease construction and to seal any gaps. Stone masonry need not be made with mortar if the stones fit together well enough, but "dry stone" walling techniques are normally only used for fencing walls because they are not wholly weatherproof.

Cyclopean masonry
In Cyclopean masonry, named after the hugely strong Cyclops of Greek myth, vast blocks of stone were carefully carved and put together without the use of mortar. Very early Greek buildings, like the Lion's Gate at Mycenae (*c.*1300 BCE), used such extremely large blocks of stone, probably from fear that smaller blocks would not stay together.

Ashlar

Ashlar is the name given to neatly carved, rectangular blocks of stone laid in regular courses. Ashlar masonry is often made with an inner core of cement or small rubble, bound together by mortar, giving the wall great stability and saving money on the cost of carving the blocks.

Rustication

Rustication is a way of carving blocks of stone to make each block more pronounced, thus giving a three-dimensional effect to the wall surface. It can be used for whole walls, as seen here at the Thiene Palace in Vicenza, Italy, or just for details such as lower stories, corners, or openings.

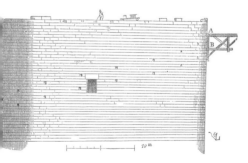

Putlogs

Medieval masonry structures were built using scaffolding supported on the building itself with a system of putlog holes. The putlogs holes were square gaps left between the blocks, into which short horizontal beams were inserted. The holes were not always filled in and therefore can sometimes still be seen today.

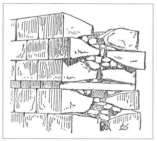

Rubble walling

It is perfectly possible to build a stone wall using small or unevenly sized pieces of stone. Such walling is known as rubble walling, and can be laid either in courses, each of a different size, or in a more random, jigsawlike pattern. Larger "through" stones are often added to the wall to provide it with greater strength.

Brick

Building blocks of dried mud were used for many millennia in hot, dry countries, but the idea of baking the mud blocks to make weatherproof bricks only developed in about the 3rd millennium BCE. Bricks were used throughout the Roman Empire, but the techniques were subsequently lost in northern Europe until the late Middle Ages. Brick was a fashionable and expensive material that was characteristic of late Gothic architecture in the Low Countries, along the Baltic coast, and also in parts of Britain. Improvements in production techniques made brick much cheaper, and it became the main house-building material during the 18th and 19th centuries in England.

Roman brick

You can easily recognize Roman bricks because they are longer and narrower than modern bricks. Although Italian buildings were often made entirely of brick, in northern parts of the Empire brick was frequently mixed with local stone to create decorative banded effects, like these arches in the theater at Lillebone, France.

Brick with stone detailing

Brick was commonly used in the timber-poor regions along the North Sea and the Baltic coasts for elaborate buildings like the Armory in Gdansk, Poland (1602–05). Stone dressings provided sculptural details that were not possible in brick, and formed a pleasing contrast between the light stone and the darker brick.

Shaped brick

Late medieval brick-makers constructed elaborately shaped bricks that could be put together to create complicated patterns and shapes, such as those on the chimneys at Thornbury Castle, Gloucestershire, England (c.1514). Shaped bricks were also used for arches, doors, and windows in this period.

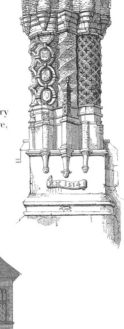

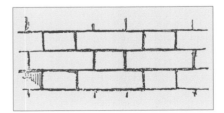

Bonds

Alternating bricks with the long side (stretcher) and short side (header) outward creates a stronger wall, and forms patterns called bonds. Flemish bond, seen here, has headers and stretchers in each row; English bond alternates header and stretcher courses and American bond has one row of headers to several of stretchers.

Polychrome brick patterns

The color of bricks depends largely on the type of clay used, but the firing temperature also affects it. Industrial processes have largely eliminated unintentional variations, but medieval and early Modern builders exploited them to create decorative polychrome (multicolored) effects, like the diagonal diaper patterns on this dovecote.

Decorative Masonry

Architects and builders have long exploited combinations of materials, both for structural purposes and to create interesting decorative effects. Masonry comes in many different colors and textures, which combine well together. Stone can also be used in combination with other materials, notably brick, to reinforce weak areas and to create an elegant contrast in textures and colors. Polychrome, or multicolored, masonry effects have been particularly popular in all periods because they are easily achieved by combining different colors of similar materials; but the variation in textures that is made possible by combining dissimilar materials can also be used to create striking effects.

Polychrome masonry
Decorative effects can be achieved by using a variety of different-colored stones, as seen here at S. Pietro in Pavia, Italy, where both the arches and the spandrels are picked out in alternating light and dark blocks. The use of polychrome masonry is particularly associated with Italy, but is also found elsewhere.

Lesenes

The English pre-Norman (Anglo-Saxon) tower at Earls Barton, Northamptonshire has a decorative pattern of raised long and short strips known as lesenes. They may be intended to imitate decorative timber framing, and probably had plaster infill between the strips, creating a more decorative effect and covering the rubble masonry walling.

Cosmati work

The Cosmatis were a 12th- and 13th century Roman family of craftsmen specializing in complex inlaid patterns using marble, glass, gilding, and mosaic for an extremely rich and beautiful effect. Cosmati work was used on many surfaces, including floors, shrines, and even columns, as here in St. John Lateran, Rome.

Flint flushwork

When flint is knapped or split, it has a dark, shiny surface. Late medieval English masons working in East Anglia, where other stone is rare, used knapped flints to infill tracery patterns and other motifs made in more expensive white limestone, creating a two-tone effect that is known as flint flushwork.

Stone quoins

Brickwork is often decorated with stone blocks or quoins at the corners and around the windows. The quoins help to reinforce the corners and also provide a decorative finish. Quoins were additionally used to reinforce the corners of stone-built walls where the blocks were either small or irregularly sized.

Wood

Wood was the most common domestic building material in Britain, northern France, Germany, Scandinavia, North America, and other heavily forested countries, and still remains popular in many areas today. Traditional timber framing is held together by carefully cut mortise-and-tenon joints and wooden pegs, but nails have commonly been used since the early 19th century. Modern framed buildings are normally clad in other materials, such as wooden siding externally and plaster internally concealing the frame, but historically the frame was often left exposed. In recent years there has been renewed interest in the more traditional methods of timber construction, in particular exposed timber framing.

Decorative framing
Different types of framing are associated with different regions, and these variations can be used to identify the location of the building. Moreton Old Hall in Cheshire, dating from *c.*1590, has the distinctive close-patterned decorative framing that is typical of northwest England.

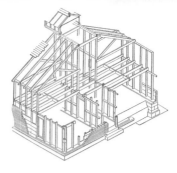

Construction

Timber framing is strong because it is composed of horizontal beams or plates supported by upright studs reinforced by diagonal braces. This modern framed house uses much smaller timber than was the case in the Middle Ages, although the framing principles are the same. The exterior is being covered in horizontal wooden siding.

Half-timbering

Half-timbering is a term sometimes used for buildings like this medieval English house in York, which has a stone lower story with timber framing above. It is also sometimes applied to buildings where the frame is exposed and the spaces between the timbers are filled with other materials such as plaster or brick.

Jetty

The upper stories of traditional timber-framed buildings were often constructed using a cantilevered projection called a jetty that brought the upper floors out beyond the lower floor. Jetties save space at ground level, but they were also fashionable, and very fine urban houses often have more than one, displaying the owner's wealth.

Mortise-and-tenon joint

A mortise-and-tenon joint is the traditional way of joining two pieces of wood at a right angle. The tenon is inserted into the mortise or hole and secured with a peg. Empty mortises, with their distinctive peg holes, are a sign that a building has been altered in some way.

Iron & Steel

The large-scale use of metal for buildings only began in the late 18th century when cast-iron columns were developed. Both cast and wrought iron were used for large-span roofs and floors, such as those in railway stations, museums, and public buildings, but their load-bearing capacity was limited, requiring masonry walls and restricting the overall building height. Architects also experimented with the decorative possibilities of cast-iron detailing, especially for roofs and interiors. Techniques rapidly improved, and structural steel was developed in the late 19th century, enabling the introduction of self-supporting steel frames and thus the creation of very tall skyscrapers.

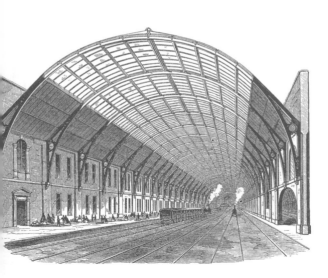

Cast-iron roof

In contrast to wood, iron was strong enough not to sag or bow, and cast iron made possible large-span roofs, such as this example at King's Cross railway station in London, built in 1851–52. It was important not to have internal columns, because if a train derailed and hit the columns, the roof would collapse.

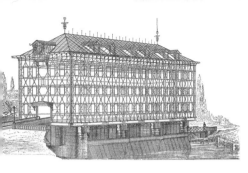

Exposed iron framing
Diagonal braces are used to create one of the earliest self-supporting iron frames in a building with floors, at the Menier chocolate factory in Noisel, France, built 1870–71. The spaces between the braces are filled with brick, but, as in the timber-framed buildings that it resembles, the brick infill is not structural.

Warehouse facade
Cast-iron facades were very fashionable in the 19th century, especially for factories and warehouses. This example from New York shows why: not only was cast iron inexpensive to model, it also had good fire resistance and could be used to create large windows and complex, yet delicate, decorative effects.

Mixed materials
The 1865–77 Vittorio Emanuel II shopping arcade in Milan, Italy makes good use of the structural and decorative possibilities of iron in combination with both stone and glass. The richly detailed facades of the stores and the premises above are complemented by the complex ironwork tracery of the fully glazed roof.

Early skyscraper
One of the first fully steel-framed buildings was the American Surety Building, New York, of 1894–96. The Maine granite exteriors act as a curtain wall and do not support the building. Originally 23 stories, it also has innovative caisson foundations that are sunk rather than dug, to lessen disturbance to the neighboring buildings.

Concrete

Concrete is made from a mixture of lime mortar, water, sand, and small pebbles or stone chips, sometimes combined with volcanic dust or ash, which is molded in wooden forms and left to harden. It is easy and cheap to make, strong, waterproof, and can be shaped to make almost anything. Concrete enabled the Romans to build domes and multistory buildings, and lies at the heart of almost all modern construction. Reinforced concrete, which is strengthened with iron or steel bars, was first developed in the mid-19th century, and combines the strength under pressure of concrete with the tensile strength of metal.

Roman concrete

The dome of the Pantheon in Rome (*c.*118–128 CE) is made of brick-reinforced concrete. The use of coffering not only helps to break up visually the surface of the interior of the dome, but it also helps to lighten the structure by making the shell thinner in places.

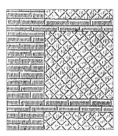

Opus reticulatum

Concrete is often covered with other materials. The Romans used a system called *opus reticulatum* to provide a good ground for finishes such as stucco render or marble facing. Square tiles or stones were set into the concrete in a diagonal netting (reticulated) pattern, sometimes in conjunction with straight bands of bricks.

Portland cement

Because it can be cast, concrete has been used since the mid-19th century for architectural details such as pediments, parapets, and balusters, which are then normally painted. The details on London's Reform Club, seen here, are carved in stone, but many other buildings used painted concrete to imitate such elements.

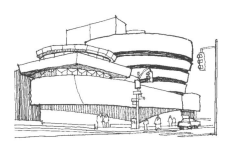

New shapes

One of the great advantages of concrete is that it can be formed into highly complex shapes. Frank Lloyd Wright's Guggenheim Museum, New York, of 1959, was one of the earliest buildings to make use of concrete to create a non-rectilinear design. Based on a nautilus shell, the structure is curved both inside and out.

Exposed concrete

Exploration of the decorative possibilities of exposed and unpainted concrete led in the 20th century to the Brutalism movement (from *béton brut*, French for "raw concrete"). Colored concrete, like the very white concrete used for the National Carillon (bell tower) in Canberra, Australia, 1970, can also be used for decorative effects.

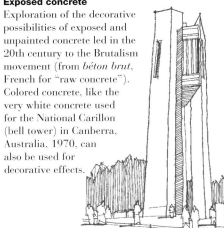

Glass

Glass is used mainly for windows, doors, and roofs in structures made in other, less breakable materials. Early glass was extremely expensive and was difficult to produce in large sizes, so individual panes of glass were small. Glass windows were used in Roman times, but then largely disappeared until the Middle Ages. Improvements in glass-making techniques in the late 18th and early 19th centuries, and the removal of harsh taxes on window glass, encouraged the use of larger windows from the mid-19th century. Further advances in building techniques, including the development of recessed curtain walls, have enabled the construction of wholly glass-clad buildings in the late 20th century.

Curtain wall
The current fashion for entirely glass-walled buildings is made possible by the curtain-wall technique. The building itself is supported by a steel and reinforced concrete frame, and the outer walls are attached to this frame and thus do not support any weight. The Bauhaus (1925–6), Dessau, Germany, is an early example.

Mosaic

The Romans developed a technique of making pictures on floors or walls out of hundreds of small, square colored glass tiles called *tesserae*, sometimes enriched with a gold-foil backing. The technique was further developed in the early Christian and Byzantine periods, creating naturalistic pictures such as these in Ravenna, Italy.

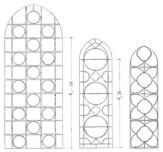

Stained-glass armature

A medieval stained-glass window is made up of numerous individual pieces of different-colored glass. These are held together with strips of lead called cames, and additional support for the glass is provided by an iron framework, or armature, which itself often forms part of the window's design.

Small-paned window

The small panes, held together by lead strips, of late medieval and early modern windows were necessitated by the difficulty of making larger pieces of glass. The numerous, and extremely expensive, glass windows of a large, late English 16th-century house like Wollaton Hall displayed the wealth of its owners, the Willoughbys.

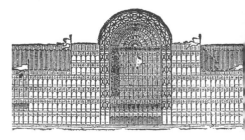

Cylinder glass

The enormous glass-and-iron Crystal Palace, built for London's 1851 Great Exhibition, used more than 900,000 square feet of industrially made cylinder glass set within a cast-iron frame. It helped to popularize smaller-scale conservatories for private houses. Moved to south London in 1854, Crystal Palace burned down in 1936.

Roofing

Roofing material needs to be weatherproof and durable, because keeping the inside of a building dry is the key to its long-term structural stability. Within these parameters, however, there is an enormous range of roofing materials, including tiles made of wood (shingles), various ceramic materials, and even stone; natural materials like thatch; metals, notably lead and corrugated iron; and various modern materials such as asphalt. The material chosen varies according to the climate. Different materials all have their own decorative qualities, and changing the roof of a building can make a huge difference to its appearance.

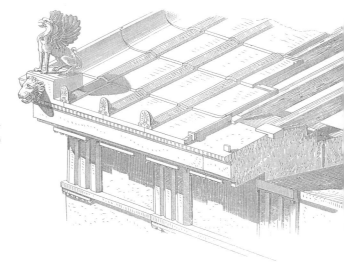

Imbrex and tegula
Greek and Roman roof tiles were made in two sections: a flat tile (*tegula*) with small raised edges covered by curved strips (*imbrices*) over the joins. The flat *tegulae* were often reused as a walling material, frequently in conjunction with stone, during the post–Roman period.

Thatch

Thatch, a thick covering of reeds or straw tightly bound together, is a surprisingly durable roofing material. It usually lasts for several decades before it needs to be replaced, and is a traditional material in many areas. Thatch tends to be very thick, and can be shaped over dormers and into decorative patterns.

Pantiles

Pantiles, which are most commonly made of orange terra-cotta and have a distinctive curved shape, were a popular roofing material throughout much of Europe. They give the roof a very distinctive corrugated appearance and their bright color is easily recognizable.

Leadwork

The use of lead roofing during the Gothic period had a huge impact on building design, enabling the construction of much flatter roofs. Unlike tiles or thatch, which must be steeply pitched in order to throw off water, lead is a continuous material and can therefore be laid on a flatter surface.

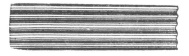

Corrugated metal

Corrugated sheet metal is an easy and cheap roofing material, although not a beautiful one. It is widely used for farm buildings and temporary structures, and is normally applied over tar paper or roofing felt, which acts as an extra barrier against moisture.

Exterior Covering

Some buildings show their underlying structure on the outside; most do not. By disguising the structure, coverings give the building a wholly different appearance. A huge variety of materials can be used as exterior wall coverings. Among the most common are plasterlike stucco (also known as render), which is often decorated with patterns, and wood. Horizontal clapboarding and weatherboarding, both also known as siding, are the most common wooden exterior wall coverings, but wooden tiles or shingles are frequently used too. There are many other coverings, including materials that imitate wood such as UPVC (vinyl), and both real and imitation stone.

Siding

You can recognize wooden siding by its distinctive pattern of horizontal strips. It may be painted, as here, or left bare to weather to an attractive gray color; cedar, pine, and oak siding are all common. In recent years, aluminum and synthetic vinyl siding has also been used.

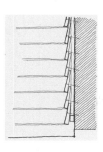
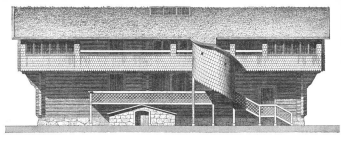

Clapboard

There are two main types of wooden siding: clapboard and weatherboard. Clapboard, seen here, was traditionally riven (split) with a tapering profile that enabled the boards to be overlapped. True weatherboarding is made of sawn boards of an even thickness; however, the two terms are often used interchangeably.

Fishscale shingle

Shingles are small wooden slabs or tiles, and may be used for roofing or as a wall covering. Like clapboard, they are thicker at one end than the other, and are usually rectangular. However, they may also be used in other shapes, like these fishscale wall shingles from Sweden.

Pargeting

In the 16th and 17th centuries timber-framed buildings were often covered with stucco, or render. This could be decorated with ornamental patterns known as pargeting. This English example from a house in Oxford has strapwork and trailing vines, but heraldic devices, geometric patterns, and figural scenes were also used.

Stone cladding

The lower story of this 1930s American home has stone cladding: thin slabs of stone (or sometimes other materials formed to look like stone) applied over a brick wall to give a more elaborate look, although the exposed brick at the side of the building gives the truth away. The upper story has simpler wooden siding.

Interior Wall Covering

The inside of a wall is usually covered with something, both to protect it and to provide a surface for decoration. The simplest interior wall covering is plain painted plaster, but plaster can also be decorated with patterns or figural scenes, covered with tapestries or wallpaper, or have raised decoration applied to it. Wooden paneling is

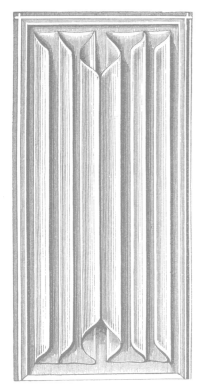

another popular interior wall covering, because it is very durable and can be made with a wide range of patterns and decorative moldings. The treatment of interior wall surfaces has changed quite considerably over time, making them a useful dating tool. Some of the main types are explored here.

Linenfold paneling

Linenfold paneling, wood that is carved to look as if it were made of very fine, folded cloth, was popular in the late 15th and 16th centuries for interior wall panels and doors. This type of paneling was revived in the 19th century as part of the craze for all things Gothic.

Wall painting

The urge for patterned wall coverings long predates the introduction of wallpaper in the 18th century. In the Romanesque and Gothic periods, scenes and patterns were painted directly onto the wall. Paintings were usually done onto dry plaster in northern Europe, and *fresco* (into wet plaster) in Italy.

Fielded paneling

This early 18th-century stairway has fielded wooden paneling. The surface is divided into separate areas, or fields, by raised moldings surrounding flat panels, thus giving the paneling its name. By dividing the wall into an upper and a lower zone, the designer has created a sense of balance and proportion.

Mixed media

Painting and sculpture can be used together to create richer, more elaborate decorative schemes, and also to differentiate between different types of figures. In the 16th-century baroque Church of the Gesù in Rome, sculpted allegorical figures representing the Virtues flank painted frescoes depicting the miracles of the saints.

Overall decoration

This 19th-century Belgian interior done in an imitation late 17th-century style has a very elaborate wall treatment, including niches, imitation marble effects, framed panels (probably intended for paintings), an intricate plasterwork cornice, and an elaborate chimneypiece. The ceiling is also heavily ornamented.

Ceiling

A ceiling is defined as the covering over the underside of the roof beams, or the underside of the floor joists in a building with more than one floor. Ceilings can be made of a wide range of materials, including metal, although wood and plaster are the most common. They may be painted with scenes and designs, or ornamented with different types of moldings made of plaster or carved wood and shaped into patterns. The joint between the wall and the ceiling is often concealed with a molded plaster or carved wooden cornice (crown molding).

Painted wooden ceiling
Not all medieval cathedrals were vaulted. The nave of Peterborough Cathedral in England has an early 13th-century wooden ceiling that is painted with the signs of the zodiac and other images. Recently cleaned and restored, it is a rare survival of a type of ceiling that was once probably much more common.

Exposed beam

In smaller medieval houses, the undersides of the floor beams were often left exposed as a decorative ceiling. These beams could be just as richly carved as their stone counterparts. This ceiling has cable and billet moldings and an elaborate boss with stylized leaf forms enriched with paint.

Coffering

Coffering is an allover pattern of recessed squares that was first used in the Roman period and was revived in the Renaissance. It is particularly used for ceilings, vaults, and dome interiors. Both the frames of the squares and the centers are usually ornamented, giving a very rich effect.

Plaster cornice

Elaborate plaster cornices were an important part of 18th- and 19th-century interiors, and helped to disguise the structural junction between wall and ceiling. This late 19th-century example uses neoclassical motifs, such as modillions and fielded panels, as well as bands of leaves, pearl beading, and anthemion with palmette.

Ceiling rose

Most 19th-century houses had decorative plasterwork in the middle of the ceiling as well as around the edges. In particular, light fittings were suspended from a decorative plaster medallion called a ceiling rose. Most ceiling roses were round, but more complex shapes, such as the one shown here, were also used.

Flooring

Floors are a fundamental part of a building and one that is easy to overlook as we walk in search of other features. At its most basic, a floor need be no more than earth pounded hard to make it solid, and earthen floors can be surprisingly dry and pleasant underfoot. Other materials like wood, tiles, and stone flagstones are more durable and lend themselves to decorative patterns and designs; they are also suitable for use on upper stories. Certain types of flooring are associated with certain periods and styles, such as mosaic, which is particularly characteristic of Roman and early Christian buildings.

Mosaic

Mosaic floors with elaborate scenes and pictures were very popular with the Romans and early Christians. This early Christian church has an elaborate mosaic floor laid out in a series of complex geometric and floral patterns. The walls above and around the altar are also covered in mosaics with figural patterns.

Earthen

This medieval great hall, an all-purpose eating, sleeping, and cooking room, most probably had a beaten earth floor. Rushes mixed with sweet-smelling herbs would have been laid on top of it to provide a soft covering underfoot; these were renewed a couple of times a year.

Medieval tiling

Tiles were a popular flooring material in the Middle Ages for churches and grand residences. Both geometric and figural patterns were common, and individual tiles were often made so that they created interlocking patterns, as here. Different colored glazes were used to enhance the patterns and create complex designs.

Scagliola

Scagliola is a colored paste made of plaster, colored pigment, and size or glue. It can be polished to a marblelike gloss. *Scagliola* was very fashionable in the 17th and 18th centuries, and was used to make imitation marble walls and patterned floors, like this one designed by the Scottish neoclassical architect Robert Adam.

Bathroom tiling

Indoor plumbing, and regular bathing, only became common during the 19th century. The discovery of germs at around the same time led to a stress on hygiene and on easily cleanable tiled surfaces for bathrooms and kitchens. Here, small mosaic tiles create an entirely washable surface on both floors and walls.

Introduction

A column is a vertical shaft. Columns are most frequently used in a row supporting a horizontal lintel (a colonnade) or with a series of arches (an arcade), but they may also be used on their own, perhaps to support a statue. They are often round, but may be square or polygonal. The transition between the column and the floor is usually aided by a base, and that with the wall above by a capital. Both bases and capitals help to spread the load, making the column more stable; they also provide a visual transition point between vertical and horizontal.

Commemorative column
The Romans used freestanding columns to commemorate great men and heroic deeds. Trajan's Column in Rome (*c.*112 CE) commemorates the Roman emperor's victory over the Dacians. The form reappeared during the neoclassical period for monuments like Nelson's Column in London and the July Column in Paris's Place de la Bastille.

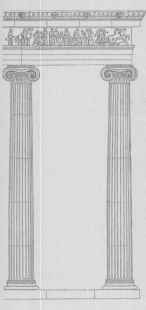

Column drums

Columns often look as if they are made of a single long stone, but in fact most are constructed from large segments or drums. A column made from just one piece of stone is called "monolithic," and the French term *en délit* is also used for the small monolithic columns common in Gothic architecture.

Pilaster

Pilasters are tall, flat strips with capitals and bases that are attached to the wall, giving the impression of columns, but performing no structural function. Here at the Temple of Bacchus at Baalbek in Lebanon (2nd century CE), they are used with an entablature, but they can also be used with arches.

Corbel

A capital that is fixed to the wall and used without an underlying column is known as a corbel. In the Romanesque and Gothic periods corbels were used to provide support for roofs, vaults, arches, and statues. This Scottish corbel from Melrose Abbey supports a small colonnette that is part of a vault respond.

Volute

The projecting knobs on the upper corners of some capitals are called volutes, and help to make the transition between the pier and the wall above. Volutes were often carved as curling foliage, but more stylized shapes (including grotesque heads) were also used, as here on this Renaissance capital.

Classical Orders

The design and proportion of columns in ancient Greece and Rome were governed by a set of rules known as the Orders. There are five main Orders: Doric, Tuscan, Ionic, Corinthian, and Composite. The Orders were rediscovered during the Renaissance and were codified by Leon Battista Alberti in his 1452 treatise *De re aedificatoria* (*On the Art of Building*), one of the key theoretical texts of the Renaissance. Each Order was considered to have particular characteristics, making them suitable for certain types of buildings. The relatively plain Doric Order, for instance, was associated with strength, while the Corinthian Order was deemed to be particularly beautiful.

Doric

You can easily recognize the Doric Order by its frieze with alternating plain or sculpted metopes and grooved triglyphs. The triglyphs represent the stylized beam ends of a timber roof. The capitals are very simple, and some early examples of the Greek Doric Order have no base.

Tuscan

The Tuscan Order, a mainly Italian type, is not dissimilar to the Doric Order, but the frieze is plain and the capitals are a little more complex, with convex astragal moldings. This Order was popular in the Renaissance, and a large-scale version of Tuscan is called the Gigantic Order.

Ionic

You can distinguish the Ionic Order by its characteristic scrolled capitals, which are said to look like a rolled-up pillow. The fronts and sides are different, unlike the other Orders. The columns are usually fluted, and the frieze may be plain or decorated with sculpted ornament.

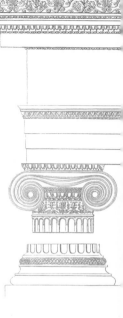

Corinthian

The Corinthian Order has capitals covered in rows of acanthus leaves, with those at the corners curling over to become volutes. There are both Greek and Roman versions: the shaft of a Greek Corinthian column is usually fluted, while that of the Roman version is plain.

Composite

The Composite Order is a particularly Roman invention, and it is the richest and most elaborate of the Orders. This Order is a cross between the Corinthian and the Ionic, with both acanthus leaves and scrolls. The frieze and entablature of this Order are also richly embellished with relief sculpture.

Early Christian

Large numbers of new churches were constructed when Christianity became the official religion of the Roman Empire in 326 CE. Most followed the aisled basilica plan (derived from a Roman civic building type) and thus had internal arcades supported on columns. Initially, early Christian capital and column forms were much like their Roman predecessors, but new capital forms that reflected Christian iconography and symbolism were developed. As the Roman Empire eventually disintegrated under increasing pressure from barbarian invasion, shifting its political focus eastward, new architectural influences from the East became more prominent, and Byzantine architectural forms developed in wholly new and highly distinctive ways.

Eastern exuberance

The Eastern influences and rich inventiveness of post-Roman Christian architecture are seen in the 6th-century churches of S. Apollinare and of S. Vitale, both in Ravenna, Italy. The main nave arcade columns are marble with "windswept" foliage capitals derived from, but not copying, the Corinthian form, while the respond capital has rich layers of leaf forms.

Ionic colonnade

In this basilica, a colonnade of Ionic columns supporting a deep entablature has been adapted to serve as a Christian church. This creates a very rich, but restrained, effect that is much closer to its Classical precedents than later, Eastern-influenced work.

Spolia

The presence of *spolia* (reused materials) explains the slightly awkward appearance of this capital from St. Demetrius in Thessaloniki, Greece. The main, lower part of the capital with its fine carving and imperial eagles has been reset in a new Christian context, with more crudely carved work above it.

Fold capital

This capital, from SS. Sergius and Bacchus, Constantinople (Istanbul), looks as if it has been made from a piece of fabric, gathered into folds by the column. Known as a fold capital, its textilelike pattern of foliage intertwining in a guilloche pattern, known as lacework, further enhances the effect.

Adaptation and combination

Older architectural forms were adapted to suit the new religion and its symbolism, as this capital from St. Mark's, Venice, combining acanthus leaves, volutes, and rich moldings with a central cross, shows. The very flat, yet deeply undercut, leaves are typical of Eastern-influenced work.

Romanesque

After the end of the Roman Empire, stone building techniques were largely lost in northern Europe, and those stone structures that were built were very simple compared to those constructed under the Romans. There was something of an artistic and cultural renaissance in the late 10th and early 11th centuries as the end of the barbarian invasions once again made contact with the Mediterranean regions feasible. The Romanesque style was one product of this artistic renaissance, and combined earlier Roman forms—albeit in considerably simplified ways—with the more decorative repertoire of geometric patterns popular among the native tribes of northern Europe.

Colonnette

A colonnette is a small column, complete with base and capital, used decoratively rather than structurally. Colonnettes were a particular feature of Romanesque and Gothic architecture, when they adorned windows, doors, and larger columns. Here they are used on the windows of the Romanesque church of Loupiac in France.

Scallop capital

A scallop capital is a wide but shallow capital with a series of flutes like the edge of a scallop shell, giving it its name. This English column, from the nave of Islip Church, Oxfordshire, has a cylindrical core surrounded by four smaller shafts.

Historiated capital

The flat surfaces of Romanesque capitals were often decorated with figural relief sculpture to create what are known as historiated (story-telling) capitals. Among the most popular narratives were miracle stories and depictions of the Virtues and Vices. Grotesques or fanciful figures were also common forms of decoration.

Decorated column

Column shafts ornamented with geometric patterns like these are a clear clue to the Romanesque period. Spirals and zigzags were especially popular, and may have been related to spiral columns that were used at Old St. Peter's in Rome, but there was no sense that sets of columns needed to match.

Column figure

Especially in French and Spanish Romanesque architecture, the columns that decorated door jambs were frequently anthropomorphized (shown in human form) as sculpted figures of saints and biblical figures. These figures, from Santiago de Compostela Cathedral in Spain, depict Old Testament prophets with scrolls.

Gothic

Standards of building and carving techniques improved enormously during the Gothic period compared to the earlier Romanesque period, and as a consequence Gothic architecture is much lighter and more delicate than Romanesque. This is particularly apparent in the carving of columns and capitals. Naturalistic foliage was very popular for capitals, and foliage predominates in the early part of the period. Columns were often created to look as if they had been made from bundles of small shafts. During the late Gothic period, capitals became extremely small, and were often little more than moldings, thus emphasizing the vertical aspect of the building.

Rich ornamentation
Early Gothic capitals, such as this 13th-century group that can be seen in Lincoln Cathedral in England, were often richly ornamented with a combination of naturalistic foliage, bold moldings, and geometric shapes like the so-called dogtooth or four-petal flowers used here. The use of dark Purbeck marble for the smaller shafts adds an extra dimension of richness.

Complex column

Complex columns, seemingly constructed of bundles of shafts, were popular in Romanesque and Gothic architecture. They appear to be made up of separate pieces, but the shafts are in fact often carved from the same block of stone, giving the column added stability and strength.

Detached shaft

This column, from the 13th-century English Gothic cathedral in Salisbury, has a round central core surrounded by four detached shafts. These detached or, *en délit*, shafts are held in place by the base and capital, and by shaft rings, special curved pieces of stone that are bonded into the main core.

Dying molding

Capitals are not necessary to join an arch to a column or wall. During the Gothic period, so-called dying moldings were sometimes used as an alternative to capitals. These taper off into the wall or column without an intervening capital, as shown in this late 13th- or early 14th-century example.

Molded capital and base

During the late Gothic period, designers moved away from exuberant foliage to simpler polygonal capitals and bases decorated with many small moldings. Columns became complex groups of tiny shafts, giving the architecture a strongly vertical feeling, as in England's Winchester Cathedral (top) and Canterbury Cathedral (bottom).

Renaissance & Baroque

A key aspect of the Renaissance was the revival of the strictly defined Classical Orders in place of more fanciful Gothic forms, which were not governed by any particular set of rules. The Tuscan and Corinthian Orders were especially popular in the Renaissance, as they were seen as most closely evoking the glories of ancient Rome. Italian Renaissance architects based designs on the ruins of ancient buildings, although they also designed some new variations on the Orders, especially the Corinthian Order, to suit their purposes. During the baroque and rococo periods, architects became more inventive, moving further away from older models to design new forms of capitals and columns.

Hierarchy of Orders
The different Orders were thought to have different visual properties, with the simple Doric and Tuscan Orders being particularly associated with strength and the Corinthian with beauty. The facade of the Rucellai Palace in Florence, for instance, has Doric pilasters on its lower story and Corinthian pilasters above.

Renaissance pilaster

This Renaissance pilaster from a Venetian church is based on the Corinthian Order, but the traditional acanthus-leaf decoration is restricted to the corners of the capital, with a more naturalistic rose at the center. The fluting on the pilaster has been replaced with foliage trails.

Banded column

Renaissance architects experimented with new forms that built on Classical ideas. One was the banded column, in which alternate blocks were larger and rusticated. Created by the French royal architect Philibert de l'Orme (*c.*1510–1570), banded columns were important in later Renaissance and baroque architecture.

Rococo capital

Rococo architects designed new forms of capitals with light decoration that suited the delicacy of the rococo style. This capital, which is almost cylindrical in shape, has little to do with the Corinthian Order on which it is nominally based, but that does not detract from its decorative potential.

Decorative column

Baroque architects used columns as decoration, as much as structural elements. The columns on the facade of the church of St. Paul and St. Louis in Paris, for instance, rest improbably on a pediment, but they add greatly to the very rich decorative effect, along with the elaborate surface ornament.

Revival Styles

In the mid-18th century scholars began studying ancient architecture in great detail, making careful drawings that were published and widely distributed. In particular, scholars such as James "Athenian" Stuart (1713–1788) and Nicholas Revett (1720–1804) brought Greek architecture to prominence, and their work was largely responsible for making accurate reproductions of ancient buildings widely available. Greek architecture was seen as having a purity that was lacking in later Roman buildings, and was also considered especially suitable for newly democratic countries such as the United States and France. Revival styles generally copied older models, but more recently architects have made interesting experiments with the columnar form, especially in relation to very tall buildings.

Antiquarian study, Ionic Order
Publications from the 18th-century provided great detail about real examples, such as this Ionic Order from Ilissus, Greece. This enabled architects to copy older models precisely, leading to a new emphasis on historical accuracy and to an expanded repertoire of forms, as previously unknown buildings were discovered and drawn.

Baseless Doric

The Greek Doric Order, which has no base and has heavier columns than the Roman type, was a great revelation to 18th-century architects and scholars. It was seen to represent a pure Classicism, untainted by the supposed decadence of Rome, and was an important feature of Greek Revival–style buildings like the Ohio State Capitol.

Skyscraper column

Early skyscrapers, like the American Surety Building in New York (1894–96), were designed to resemble enormous freestanding columns. The lower stories represented the base, the upper stories with the projecting cornice was the capital, and the vertical rows of windows formed a kind of fluting on the "shaft."

Britannic Order

In the neoclassical period the discovery of variations on the Orders led 18th-century architects to experiment with designing new Orders. The Britannic Order, seen here, includes the British royal lion and unicorn, while the US Capitol in Washington, DC was adorned with a "corncob" Order, which has ears of corn in place of acanthus leaves.

Pipe column

In the 20th century, Modernist architects abandoned bases and capitals in favor of plain columns that clearly expressed their function with no superfluous ornamentation. Nonetheless, columns remained useful for support and to give rhythm to the facade, as here at Le Corbusier's Villa Savoye, Poissy, France, of 1929–31. Similar concrete-covered or concrete-filled pipe columns are often used to support basements.

Introduction

There are two main ways of spanning an opening: with a flat lintel or with a curved arch. Both lintels and arches can be supported on freestanding columns or incorporated into a wall, but arches are stronger than lintels because the curve helps to angle the downward forces into the wall or column. The Greeks used a trabeated or beamed system of construction with a flat lintel or entablature supported on columns, but the Romans exploited the structural possibilities of the arch to create larger, more complex buildings. Nonetheless, they retained the visual device of an entablature and columns superimposed around an arch.

Trabeated construction
The Greeks used the trabeated or beamed system of construction, in which openings are spanned by horizontal lintels supported by columns. Because the lintel is relatively weak, the columns must be close together to support it, resulting in the tightly spaced arcades characteristic of Greek architecture.

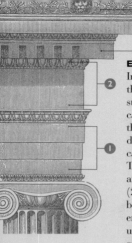

Entablature

In Classical architecture, the entire horizontal structure above the capitals, including the lintel and any decoration above it, is called the entablature. This includes the architrave (1), the frieze (2), and the cornice (3) below the roof. The entablature can also be used by itself as a form of decoration.

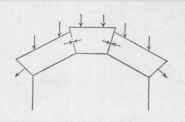

Keystone

The keystone at the center of an arch is literally the key that locks the arch into place. As this diagram shows, the blocks, or *voussoirs*, around the arch are cut at an angle. The keystone at the top is angled on both sides to lock the structure together.

Roman arch

Arches were not invented by the Romans, but they were the first to truly exploit their decorative and structural possibilities. Roman arches were normally round, as here in the Arch of Constantine in Rome, and were often combined with a heavy entablature and pilasters, relegating the arch itself to a subsidiary visual position.

Supportive arch

The Romans also exploited the ability of the arch to withstand downward pressure in order to build multistory buildings. This cutaway view of the Colosseum in Rome shows how arches were used to support the upper floors. The very thick outer walls in turn acted as buttresses to help support the arches.

Shape

When we speak of something being arched, we are usually describing a curved shape. In architecture, arches come in a multitude of variants on a curve; architectural arches may also, surprisingly, be flat, but all structural arches share the characteristic of being composed of shaped blocks of stone laid in such a way that they are structurally stable. Arch shapes changed over time, and certain shapes are characteristic of certain periods. The most common shapes, however, are the round or semicircular arch, which is associated with the Roman, Romanesque, and Renaissance periods, and the pointed arch, which is characteristic of the Gothic period.

Round

The individual blocks, or *voussoirs*, around these round-arched Romanesque windows are cut in wedge shapes along angles that follow the radius of the arch, an arrangement known as radial *voussoirs*. This means that each block presses downward against its neighbor and is therefore supported.

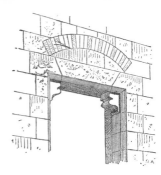

Flat

In a flat arch, the individual blocks across the top of the arch are angled so that they press against each other, rather than down. Flat arches are commonly used in brick buildings to create the straight openings over windows and doors characteristic of the Georgian and Victorian periods.

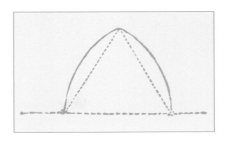

Pointed

A pointed arch is formed by two segments of a circle joined together, creating curved sides and a point at the top. The great advantage is that the angle at the top is almost infinitely adjustable, enabling the arch to be widened or narrowed easily without compromising its height.

Horseshoe

Horseshoe arches, which are more than semicircular, are particularly characteristic of the architecture of Islam, including that of Islamic-period Spain, as here at the church of Sta. Maria la Blanca, Toledo, built in the 12th century as a synagogue and converted to a church in c.1405.

Shouldered

"Shouldered arch" is a term that is used to describe an opening of the shape seen in this window, which looks like a stylized neck and shoulders. It is not, however, a true arch composed of shaped blocks, but a straight lintel that is resting on corbels at the top of the opening.

Romanesque

Romanesque architecture, which was the dominant style in western Europe between the 10th and 12th centuries, is characterized by the use of round arches. The earliest Romanesque arches were very plain, but several Orders or rows of arches could be used together to create a richer effect. In the 12th century increasing amounts of ornament were used, and arches were decorated with roll moldings, chevrons, and other geometric ornament, giving a rich, but somewhat barbaric look. Arches were also used as decorative features, notably in the form of blind arcades, carved so that they opened only onto the wall and not into a separate space.

Nave arcade

It is noticeable how early Romanesque architecture was often very plain and massive, gaining its beauty from strength rather than elaborate ornament. This nave arcade, for instance, has three almost plain arches of diminishing size, which are ornamented only with the slightest chamfer on the edges, visually decreasing the weight of the arches without compromising their strength.

Giant Order

A Giant Order—a large-scale arch that encloses other arches or Orders within it—was commonly used during the Romanesque period. It gave vertical unity to elevations that were otherwise very horizontal, as can be seen here at Jedburgh Abbey in Scotland, where a Giant Order encloses both the nave and the gallery arcades.

Geometric ornament

In the later Romanesque period, earlier plainness gave way to a wide variety of geometric ornament—often, as seen here, combining several motifs on the same opening. These arches in St. Peter's Church, Northampton, England, are decorated with a variety of different types of chevron or zigzag ornament.

Blind arcading

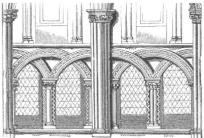

Decorative or blind arcading was a common feature in the Romanesque period, and was often made in the form of two intersecting arcades. The pointed arches created where round arches meet, as here at St. Cross, Hampshire, England, may have encouraged the development of pointed arches in the subsequent Gothic period.

Clasping motif

Romanesque masons and sculptors delighted in fanciful or grotesque motifs. Here, stylized animals with large snouts on one part of an arch are chomping down on a roll molding below. Similar clasping motifs with bird heads (known as beak heads) and with chevron moldings are also common.

Gothic

The pointed arch became popular in Western architecture in the 12th century and is the key component, both structurally and decoratively, of Gothic architecture. Pointed arches are visually lighter, though structurally stronger, than round arches, because the blocks at the top of the arch press inward against each other rather than downward. This enabled Gothic masons to build lighter and seemingly more delicate buildings than had been possible with round arches. Initially, pointed arches were relatively tall and narrow, but in the late Gothic period masons experimented with new forms, including the S-shaped ogee arch and the flatter four-centered arch.

Pointed arch
Gothic masons exploited the structural stability of the pointed arch to build very large, tall buildings, like Cologne Cathedral in Germany. Not only are the arches of the arcades pointed, but the windows, window tracery, and vaults all exploit pointed arches for added stability. The buttresses, too, are pointed half-arches.

Multiple moldings

Gothic arches are often ornamented with very fine moldings forming a series of rolls and hollows, giving the arch a more delicate appearance than had been the case in the earlier Romanesque period. Although each molding seems separate, they are actually all carved together on the same *voussoir* blocks.

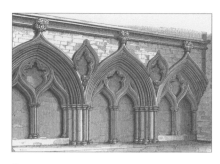

Ogee

The ogee arch, which has a reverse, or S-shaped, curve at its top, was an important aspect of Gothic architecture in the 14th century. It enabled the creation of sinuous curves and interlocking patterns, such as the teardrop shapes formed in this blind arcading in Norwich Cathedral, England.

Four-centered arch

Four-centered arches are named for the four compass points required to draw them: one for each corner, and two for the center section. Frequently called Tudor arches, they are a key element in English late Gothic architecture. Often surrounded by a square hood molding, the spandrels created were filled with decorative carving.

Cusping

This late Gothic arch has cusping: small, decorative points projecting from the curve of the arch. These are formed by the use of small curves set within the larger arch; where the curves meet, they form a point, or cusp. The curves may themselves be cusped, as here, for even greater elaboration.

Renaissance & Baroque

Beginning in 15th-century Italy and slowly spreading northward, the Renaissance brought with it a revival of interest in the architecture of ancient Rome, and Gothic forms (notably the pointed arch) were abandoned. Instead, architects revived the round arch and the entablature carried on pilasters. In contrast to the original Roman models, however, greater emphasis was placed on the arch itself, and both arches and arcades were occasionally used on their own, without a surrounding entablature. New forms of the arch, including arches without capitals, rusticated arches, and arches supported on an entablature, were also developed.

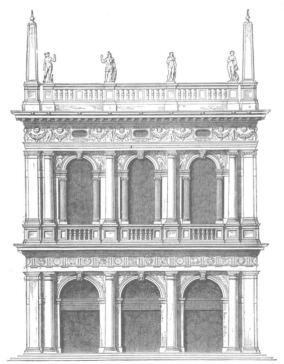

Arches and entablature

The Roman motif of a round arch set under an entablature supported on pilasters was also a hallmark of Renaissance architecture. Here, on the Old Library of St. Mark's, Venice, begun in 1537, the two layers of entablature provide a strongly rectilinear frame that dominates the arches.

Rusticated arch

Arches formed from rusticated blocks without clearly defined capitals were another hallmark of Renaissance architecture. The lower story of this 16th-century Italian villa designed by Andrea Palladio has only the barest suggestion of an arcade, with rusticated arches and heavy rusticated piers between the windows.

Depressed arch

Gothic and Renaissance were less clearly differentiated in northern Europe than in Italy. For instance, the open lower story of the Braunschweig Cloth Hall in Germany combined very depressed arches similar to late Gothic Tudor arches with a Renaissance entablature and pilasters. Similar arches were used in the upper stories.

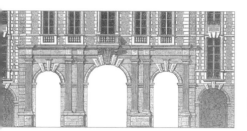

Blocked keystone

Blocked keystones, so named because the individual blocks are so clearly delineated, were a fashionable Renaissance motif. The entrances into the 17th-century Place Royale in Paris have three round-headed arches with very prominent keystones that extend well beyond the moldings around the arch.

Loggia

A loggia is a long covered space with an open arcade along one side, which may be part of the building or separate. A particularly Italian form, loggias were also used in other countries in order to evoke Italian architecture. Here, at the Ospedale Grande, Milan (begun 1456), there are two levels of loggias, one situated above the other.

Revival Styles

Architects working in the various 18th- and 19th-century revival styles all made use of arches and entablatures as necessary to convey an impression of their chosen style. As a consequence, an entablature supported on a colonnade became a kind of shorthand for the (neo)Classical style, and pointed arches could similarly be used to imply the Gothic Revival. There were also some attempts in the 19th century to develop new styles, one of the most interesting of which was the *Rundbogenstil*, or round-arched style. Drawing on aspects of all the round-arched styles, it made much of their decorative possibilities.

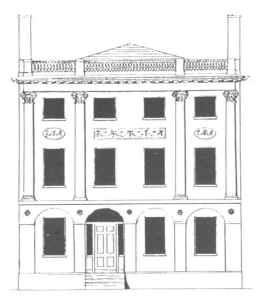

Neoclassical house
The entablature supported by a colonnade was an intrinsic decorative feature of neoclassical architecture. In this early 19th-century American house, the roof cornice is treated like an entablature with four decorative pilasters supporting it. The lower story is articulated with an arcade linking the windows and off-center door.

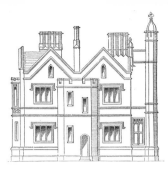

Gothic Revival style

The small pointed-arched windows and door, and the use of tracery, give this early 19th-century house a Gothic Revival flavor, which is further enhanced by the pointed gables, irregular chimneys, and crenellated staircase turret at the front, and by the tall turret at the side.

Rundbogenstil

The *Rundbogenstil* (round-arched style) was an eclectic 19th-century revival style. Always built in masonry, like this church in Ann Arbor, Michigan, it combines elements from many round-arched styles including early Christian, Romanesque, and Renaissance, and is characterized by heavy arches and chunky rustication.

Triumphal arch

Bloomingdale's department store in New York, opened in 1886, uses the motif of a Roman triumphal arch for its entrance. Spanning the lower two stories of the facade, the central arch and narrower vertical panels—like the massive side sections of a triumphal arch—are defined by heavy rusticated pilasters.

Gothic Revival porch

The cusped arch on stylized Gothic columns over the entrance to this 1870s Gothic Revival porch is a key stylistic signal. Its details are mirrored in the decorative arches and roundels on the door itself, but the detailing seems applied rather than a fundamental part of the structure.

Modern

Neither arches nor entablatures lost their place in 20th-century architecture. Arches were (and continue to be) a structurally important component of new building types, especially those related to transport, such as train stations and airports, because their strength enables the construction of the very large, open spaces necessary to accommodate huge crowds. Steel framing is constructed using a trabeated system, and Modernist architects have embraced its visual possibilities to create stripped-down colonnades. The concepts of the colonnade and the arcade have also proved useful as a way of creating long stretches of visually unified shop fronts, such as those along London's Regent Street.

Train station
The giant arches that are characteristic of 19th-century railway stations are functional and decorative. The inherent strength of arches enabled giant glass-and-iron barrel-vaulted roofs to be built over the train lines; these were expressed on the outside through huge arches like these on the front of King's Cross station in London.

Rusticated arcade

In designing his row of shops and offices for London's Regent Street in 1923, the architect Reginald Blomfield drew on classical precedents like Renaissance *palazzos* and loggias to create a street-level arcade. The arches themselves have no capitals—only heavy keystones and very prominent rustication.

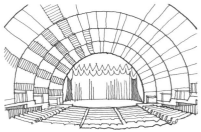

Art Deco arch

The arch was an important form in Art Deco architecture, and was used both decoratively and structurally, as here at Radio City Music Hall in New York (opened in 1932). Its proscenium arch (*proscenium* being Greek for "in front of the stage") uses concentric arches to provide a feeling of depth and grandeur.

Modernist arcade

The screen of columns across the front of New York's Lincoln Center (1962) is inspired by Greek temple facades, but the very clean lines, without ornament, are wholly Modern. The slightly curved arches of each bay of the main arcade are reflected in the lower story and in the Center's tapering columns.

Parallel arch

The arch has become an important part of very recent architecture, as architects have experimented with novel ways of using modern materials. Sydney Opera House in Australia uses parallel arches to create large spaces with a distinctive profile and excellent acoustics.

Introduction

The roof is the feature that makes a structure a building, rather than just some walls around an open space. At its most basic, a roof must keep out the weather, and so roofs (even so-called flat roofs) are usually angled to enable water to drain off. Flat roofs are more common in dry climates, while in more severe climates steeply pitched roofs are the norm. Roof shapes are also used by architects to create certain building styles, with flat roofs being associated with the Italian Renaissance and steeply pitched ones with the Middle Ages and the French Renaissance.

Pitched roof
A pitched, or triangular, roof is the most basic shape and one of the easiest to make. It sheds water easily and lends itself to many different types of coverings. The triangular bit of wall supporting the roof at either end is called a gable.

Overhanging eaves

The roof of this Swiss house projects to create overhanging eaves, helping to keep snow and rain from falling immediately around the house. Deep eaves are also common in hot climates because they help to shelter the walls from the sun.

Heraldic battlements

These distinctive swallowtail crenellations have a symbolic purpose that goes beyond mere decoration. This shape was used to denote the owner's allegiance to the Guelph party, one of the main political factions in late medieval Verona, Italy. Guelph rivalry with the Ghibelline party inspired Shakespeare's *Romeo and Juliet*.

Catslide roof

The roof of this American house extends downward from the main slope in order to encompass an additional single-story extension in an arrangement known as a catslide, or saltbox, roof. This is an easy way of roofing two separate sections without creating a valley or gutter in between them.

Concealed roof

The concealed roof, which draws on ancient Roman precedents, was a key feature of the Italian Renaissance that was widely copied elsewhere. The roof of the Verospi Palace in Rome is very low-pitched, and so is entirely hidden from the viewer on the ground by the heavy cornice.

Classical

The most important Classical roof form was a long pitched roof ending in decorative gables or pediments. This is one of the simplest types of roof to construct, and many elements of the Classical Orders, such as metopes and triglyphs, are representations in stone of structural roof components. The proportions of height to width of a pitched roof are dependent on its size. To keep roofs from becoming too large and unwieldy, the Romans began combining a decorative facade with a flat roof concealed behind a cornice, thus enabling them to build large and complex buildings and still retain a pedimented facade.

Extended pitched roof

The typical roof shape of an ancient Greek temple, such as the Temple of Zeus Olympios, was a simple pitched roof over the length of the building, ending in decorative gables or pediments at either end. Where there was a surrounding colonnade or portico, the pitch of the roof was extended outward to cover it.

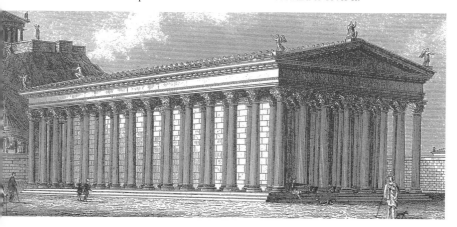

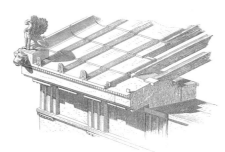

Antefix and *acroterion*

The ends of the curved *imbrex* tiles covering the joints on this roof are covered by small upright tiles called *antefixae*, which are usually ornamented with an anthemion (honeysuckle) motif. The blocks at the corners of the gable are called *acroteria*, and frequently, as shown here, carried statues.

Triglyph

Fluted triglyph panels were a distinctive part of the Doric Order. This diagram shows how they probably developed as representations in stone of the ends of roof beams, with the flat metopes in between being the spaces between the beams. The flat frieze immediately below represented the lintel beam.

Sculpted pediment

Carved figures of deities and religious stories were an important part of the decoration of both Classical temples and Christian churches. The pediment of the Parthenon in Athens, for instance, seen here in a reconstruction, was filled with sculpted reliefs of the battle between the gods and the giants of Greek mythology.

Pedimented facade and flat roof

Pediments must become higher as they become wider to maintain their proportions, potentially making them very large and unwieldy. The early 1st-century CE Temple of Concord in Rome shows how the Romans combined a pedimented facade with a flat roof to create a larger building, setting a precedent for later design.

Romanesque

In the Romanesque period, roofs were ordinarily visible, rather than being hidden behind a parapet or balustrade, and their long slopes formed an important part of the visual aesthetic of the period's architecture. Steeply pitched roofs, conical and polygonal shapes all appear, and were used according to the shape of the structure they covered. The layering of different roof shapes was an important part of the visual massing, especially in churches where each of the compartmentalized spaces required a separate roof. Gable ends were also prominently decorated with sculpture and complicated window arrangements, making the gable a key element of Romanesque facade design.

Multiple roof styles
The 12th-century cathedral at Worms in Germany has typically Romanesque roofs. The nave roof is pitched, and the aisles have lean-to roofs that rest against the nave wall. The smaller towers have conical roofs, reflecting their round shape, while the central tower and apse roofs are polygonal.

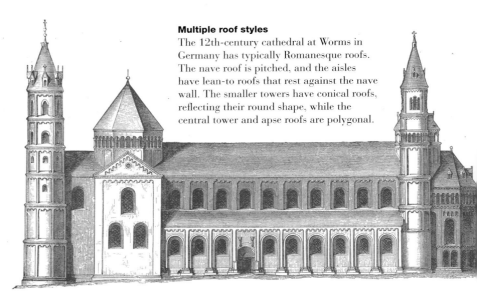

Decorated gables

The gable ends of Romanesque and Gothic churches were often heavily ornamented and formed one of the most prominent decorative features of the exterior.

The gable at the French church of Saint-Père in Vézelay, seen here, contained statues; complex window designs, especially rose windows, were also very popular for gables.

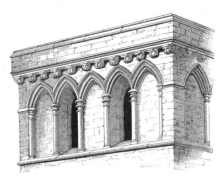

Corbel table

In the Romanesque period the edges of roofs and towers were often decorated with a line of corbels representing the ends of the roof beams carved in stone. The corbels might be carved as heads, animals, grotesque figures, or simply as different geometric shapes.

Corbelled parapet

In defensive buildings, the parapet allowed defenders to hide and shoot arrows unseen, and also helped to protect the roof from objects shot up from below. The Palazzo della Ragione gateway in Mantua, Italy, conceals its roof behind a corbelled parapet, a low wall projecting up above the roofline.

Gargoyle

The spouts used to divert rainwater over the side of the building were often turned into a grotesque animal or human form, known as a gargoyle, during the Middle Ages. Gargoyles were particularly popular in France, but are also found elsewhere.

ROOFS & GABLES
Gothic

The aesthetic of the Gothic period was much lighter and more delicate than had been the case in the earlier Romanesque period, and this was as true of roofs as it was of other parts of the building. Construction techniques also developed, enabling the construction of more complicated shapes than had previously been possible. Some of the most elaborate Gothic roofs are found in halls, the large rooms that formed the main living, sleeping, and cooking space of a medieval house. Open to the rafters, the hall's roof timbers might be elaborately decorated to show the owner's wealth and taste.

Open hall roof
The very tall, double-height windows extending almost from the ground into the roof dormers on the side of the late 13th-century hall at Stokesay Castle in Shropshire, England are a clear pointer to the nature of the roof inside. The hall must be open to the roof, because such windows would not otherwise be feasible.

Crown-post roof

The central post with braces radiating in all directions in a roof is called a crown post. It supports a central purlin with crosswise tie beams, which helps to ensure that the individual triangular trusses stay vertical and do not fall against each other like a pack of cards.

Bargeboards

Bargeboards are carved boards placed along the roof edge at the gable end of a building to cover and protect the ends of the rafters from the weather. They also provide a decorative finish, and can be plain or carved, as seen on this late 14th-century English house in Kent.

Windbraces

The shaped timbers running at an angle on the sides of this roof between the horizontal purlins and the vertical principal rafters are known as windbraces. Their name reflects their function in ensuring that the rafters stay in place and do not collapse onto each other in a high wind.

Hammerbeam roof

Here, a short horizontal beam (the hammerbeam) is cantilevered out from the wall and supports an upright hammer-post, which in turn carries the upper roof structure, creating a very wide internal span. In churches, the hammerbeam ends are sometimes decorated with angels, giving rise to the alternative name of angel roof.

Late Gothic

In the late Gothic period the increasingly widespread use of lead as a roofing material enabled the introduction of much flatter rooflines, and the use of a parapet further hid the roof from the viewer on the ground, creating a boxy silhouette outside and an almost flat ceiling inside. Openwork parapets were especially popular because they created a dramatic silhouette against the sky. Crenellated parapets of the type normally used on castles were also very fashionable, reflecting the chivalric ethos that permeated many aspects of late medieval art and architecture; and manor houses and even churches were adorned with pretend military battlements.

Changing roofline
The fashion for much flatter roofs in the late Gothic period meant that many churches had their original steeply pitched roofs altered. Here, the remains of the original steep gable line are still visible below the later, flatter roofline.

Arch braces

The introduction of flatter rooflines outside was mirrored inside by much flatter interior shapes. Here, a low-pitched roof is supported on massive tie beams, which are themselves supported by arch braces attached to the walls. Small tracery trefoils adorn the spandrels, and the undersides of the arches are cusped.

Openwork parapet

Openwork parapets constructed using unglazed tracery that showed up against the sky were popular in the late Gothic period and could be made in very elaborate patterns. This English example from a church tower in Gloucestershire is crenellated and also has openwork turrets, pinnacles, and miniature flying buttresses.

Machicolations

Machicolations are narrow slots cut in the floor of the flat area behind the parapet, which enabled defenders to shoot arrows downward or to throw objects at attackers below. The Knights' Hall at Malbork Castle in Poland has a crenellated parapet that projects outward to form machicolations over the corner turrets.

Decorative crenellations

Having crenellations on one's house, with its implications of military independence, was an important status symbol during the late Gothic period, but they were almost always decorative rather than functional. This bay window has crenellations, but any attacker would simply have smashed the large windows below.

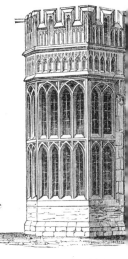

Renaissance

During the Renaissance, rooflines depended very much on the country in question, especially in the early Renaissance period. In Italy relatively low-pitched, Classically inspired roof shapes predominated, and the hipped roof, which is angled at the ends as well as the sides, was a key shape. Heavy cornices at the junction of wall and roof were also a principal element of Italian Renaissance roof design. In France very steeply pitched roofs were fashionable, while in the Low Countries and along the North Sea coast elaborately shaped gables were one of the most noticeable elements of roof design.

Multiple gables
Rows of small gables are particularly characteristic of 17th-century English architecture. This house in Oxford has gables that are placed over a series of projecting oriel windows. Unfortunately, the valleys between the gables were prone to rot, and in later years many of these multiple gables were replaced.

Shaped gables

Elaborately shaped gables are typical of northern European architecture of the later 16th and 17th centuries. All manner of shapes were possible; for instance, the armory in Gdansk, Poland, has convex and concave curves, strapwork and obelisk ornaments, and pointed pediments with urns at the top.

Elaborate combinations

Very complex rooflines are typical of French Renaissance architecture. The Château de Chambord incorporates a mixture of steeply pitched hipped roofs with conical roofs over the projecting bays, and all manner of turrets, dormers, and elaborate chimneys, giving it a multifaceted appearance.

Decorative gables

The roofs of the great English house at Longleat in Wiltshire are low-pitched and are hidden from view behind a parapet. The shaped gables, with their two smaller flanking gables over the bay windows, are simply there for decoration and to give some punctuation to the roofline.

Hipped roof

The mid-16th-century Villa Giulia in Rome, which was built for Pope Julius III, has a very low-pitched, hipped roof that is sloped on all four sides. It is crowned by a shallow lantern, and there is a heavy cornice at the junction of roof and wall.

Baroque & Rococo

In many ways the roof design of the baroque period carried on the styles of the Renaissance, notably the use of hipped roofs and heavy cornices or parapets to create a rectilinear silhouette. Shaped gables became less popular, and there was reduced regional variation, although French baroque architects continued to favor very high, steeply pitched roofs rather than the flatter roofs fashionable in Italy, England, and elsewhere. The greater emphasis on ornament in the baroque led to the development of elaborate balustrades used as parapets, often further ornamented with urns or statues at the corners. The double-pitched mansard roof was also developed in this period.

Steeply pitched roof
The mid-17th-century Château de Beaumensil has the very steeply pitched roofs with prominent dormer windows that continued to characterize French domestic architecture throughout the baroque and rococo periods. The sloping roofline combined with the lower walls gives the building a light and decorative appearance.

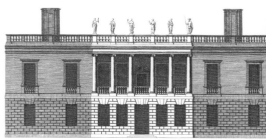

Mansard roof

The mansard roof, which is associated with the 17th-century French architect François Mansart, has a double slope on each face. The lower slope is fairly straight, often almost vertical, while the upper section is much flatter. The lower section usually has dormers, thus creating an extra story in the roof.

Balustraded parapet

The roofs of the Queen's House in Greenwich, London, of 1615–37, are entirely concealed behind a balustraded parapet. The balusters are in the vase shape then also becoming fashionable for staircases, and, like a Gothic openwork parapet, they help to lighten the impact of the parapet against the sky.

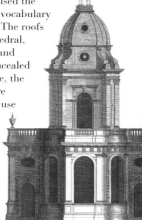

Balustrade with urns

Baroque churches used the same architectural vocabulary as other buildings. The roofs of St. Philip's Cathedral, Birmingham, England (1709–15), are concealed behind a balustrade, the corners of which are emphasized by the use of decorative urns. There is also a heavy cornice at the base of the dome.

Cornice

Decorative cornices were used to adorn the junction of roof and wall. As well as decorating the projecting eaves, the cornice, like this one on the church of St. Benet, London (1683), designed by Sir Christopher Wren, also forms an important visual termination to the wall.

Neoclassical

The neoclassical period was marked by a revival of ancient forms based on close observation of original buildings, and the porticoed temple became very popular for public buildings and even for houses. As had been the case in the Roman period, it was often combined with a larger, flat roof structure, although pure Greek temple forms were also used. Palladian architects put particular emphasis on hipped roofs, often combining them with a cupola or a central roof light enclosed in a balustrade, and hipped roofs became a key feature of domestic architecture. Substantial cornices with modillions, or console brackets, were another important part of neoclassical architecture.

Greek-style pitched roof

The Glyptothek (Greek for "sculpture gallery") in Munich (1816–30) was one of the earliest purpose-built museums. It combines a central temple form, complete with pedimented Ionic portico and pitched roof of Greek form, with two lower wings based on Italian Renaissance precedents with low roofs hidden behind parapets.

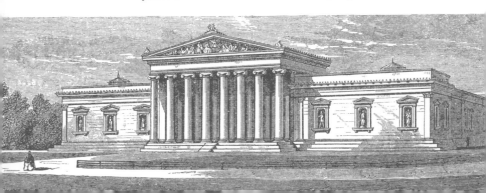

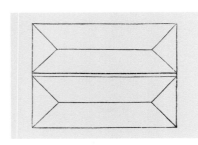

Valley roof

In order to create low roofs that still had sufficient pitch to drain off the rain, architects often used M-roofs or valley roofs. An M-roof has two adjacent low roofs that are separated by a central valley or gutter, and consequently is easy to disguise behind a parapet.

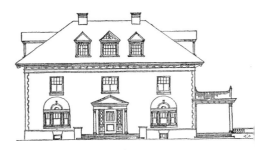

Hipped roof

This 18th-century American house has a hipped roof, angled on all four sides, with three small dormers across the front and larger dormers at the sides. The eaves project and are supported on a modillion cornice, and the two chimney stacks form punctuation marks across the ridge.

Modillion cornice

Modillions are essentially scroll-shaped console brackets used horizontally rather than vertically, and like consoles, they appear to support the roof above. The flat spaces between the modillions were often ornamented, as here, with rosettes. This cornice also has additional egg-and-dart, pearl beading, and dentil moldings.

Balustraded roof light

This design for an early 19th-century house in Virginia has a central balustraded roof light on top of a hipped roof, which illuminates the core interior space over the stairwell. At the sides, the roof and its balustrade both project outward over the side porticoes, in a similar style to a Greek temple.

Victorian & Modern

Rooflines have changed considerably over the last 200 years; 19th-century (Victorian) revival styles were largely derived from the Picturesque movement, which placed great emphasis on irregularity and variety, leading to the construction of very complex rooflines. The development of tall buildings, whose roofs could be difficult to see from the ground, led first to the use of heavily ornamented cornices and later to flat roofs. Flat roofs became popular for houses and other buildings during the 20th century, and were a key element of the Modern style, but late 20th-century Postmodernism has seen a return to more complex rooflines.

Projecting cornice
The heavy projecting cornice on the top of the Ames Building in Boston (1889–93), one of the tallest buildings of its time, gives the upper part of the building an imposing presence without the need for the actual roof to be visible. Its design is derived from Italian Renaissance models.

Steep roof

The high, steeply pitched roofs of the mid-19th-century Bourse in Lyon, France, revive French Renaissance and baroque styles, but—as is typical of many 19th-century buildings—they are actually larger, more complex and more elaborate than anything that would have been built when the style was originally in use.

Cottage orné

The complex rooflines of this early 19th-century *cottage orné*, or Picturesque cottage, which includes two different types of dormers, a complex hip at the end, and ornamental chimneys, form a key part of its design. In particular the variety was intended to give it an ornamental or picturesque quality.

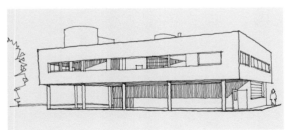

Flat roof

Modern architecture of the 20th century is characterized above all by the use of boxy shapes, including flat roofs, which stress function above all other considerations. Le Corbusier's Villa Savoye, Poissy, France, was a key building during the Modernist movement, and its flat roof forms a major part of its clean lines.

Decorative roofline

Skyscrapers are so tall that their roofs are invisible. During the late 20th century, architects moved away from the flat roofs that were popular earlier in the century to create highly decorative roofs, like this oversized broken pediment. London's tapering "Gherkin" is another example of this trend.

VAULTS Introduction

A vault is an arch projected forward to form a curved covering over an interior space. Vaults were invented in Antiquity, and were popular for Roman, early Christian, and Byzantine buildings. Their use was rediscovered in western Europe during the Romanesque period, and the invention of the pointed arch in the Gothic period enabled much larger and more elaborate vaults to be constructed. Vaults were especially popular for churches, where they symbolized the vault of heaven as well as providing a fireproof ceiling. Their strength also made them useful for cellars, undercrofts, and crypts, where they helped support the superstructure above.

Gothic rib vault
The molded ribs along the edge of each section of a rib vault provide stability as well as definition for the vault. Rib vaults, such as these 13th-century vaults at St. Gereon in Cologne, Germany, are particularly characteristic of the Gothic style. Here, the ribs spring from slender wall shafts, thereby giving the impression that the vault is an elegantly stretched canopy.

Roman barrel vault

The Romans were the first to develop vaults on a large scale. This barrel vault, which is curved in only one direction, is from the *tepidarium*, or warm room, of the Baths at Pompeii of *c.*100 BCE. It was decorated with frescoes that continued the scheme on the walls.

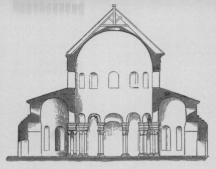

Early Christian dome

Domes are a kind of vault, projected around in a circle, rather than along a straight axis. The arched shape of the dome of the early Christian church of S. Constanza in Rome (*c.*350 CE) is clear in this section. There are barrel vaults in the surrounding aisle.

Vaulted crypt

Vaults that are composed of intersecting arches are very strong, so they were often used to strengthen lower stories such as crypts. At Gloucester Cathedral in England (*c.*1100), the large, stubby piers and thick arches of the Romanesque crypt help to support the choir above.

Vaulted ceiling

In the Renaissance and baroque periods, architects experimented with making vaulted ceilings using lath and plaster rather than the traditional solid materials. This made it possible to vault very large spans in a smooth curve, as here in the early 18th-century church of St. James Piccadilly, London.

Barrel & Groin

A barrel vault has a single curved surface running the length of the building. Commonly used during the Roman period, it is usually rounded, but can also be pointed. Barrel vaults went out of fashion during the Gothic period when rib vaults became popular, but they returned to fashion in the Renaissance because of their association with Classical Antiquity. Additional vaults can be constructed at right angles to the main vault, thereby creating a groin vault and enabling the insertion of clerestory windows in each section. Groin vaults are named after the angled edge or "groin" created where the two vaults meet. Unlike rib vaults, however, the groins are not reinforced with ribs.

Bay definition

Both barrel and groin vaults are often divided into bays or compartments by transverse arches set across the vault. These arches add stability as well as breaking the vault up visually. In the Romanesque abbey church of Saint-Père in Vézelay, France, the bay rhythm of the groin vaulting is further emphasized by the prominent shafts that are supporting the arches.

Coffered barrel vault

The baroque church of St. Peter's, Rome, built to replace the church created by the Emperor Constantine, has a barrel vault that reinterprets ancient Roman models. Richly decorated with coffering, it is pierced by clerestory windows to allow more light into the upper part of the vault, which would otherwise be very dark.

Transverse arch

This diagram of a Roman barrel vault shows how the single continuous curve of the vault is supported by transverse arches. These transverse arches rise from the piers of the aisle arcades, giving them additional thickness and stability at the base, while the string course above the arcade gives horizontal definition.

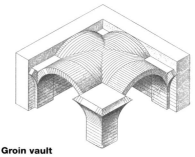

Groin vault

Looked at from above, it is easy to see how the groin vaults of the Hagia Sophia, Constantinople (Istanbul), were constructed from two intersecting barrel vaults with the intersections cut back at 45° to the main axis of the vault. The use of groin vaults permitted the addition of openings into each section.

Centering

Vaults were ordinarily constructed over wooden forms known as centering, as shown here. The centering had the shape of the underside of the finished vault, and the stones of the vault (here supporting a bridge) were laid over it from above. When the vault was complete, the centering was removed, leaving only the vault.

Rib

In the early 12th century, masons discovered that groin vaults could be strengthened by the addition of ribs along the edges of the groins. This discovery helped pave the way for the Gothic style, which is particularly characterized by the use of rib vaults. The introduction of the pointed arch around the same time further increased the architectural possibilities of the rib vault, because pointed arches can be made wider or narrower more easily than round arches, creating greater flexibility in vaulting forms. From the 13th century onward, vaults became more complex as additional decorative ribs were added.

Unifying rib
The soaring interior of the late medieval cathedral in Milan, Italy, is unified by its rib vault. The ribs draw the eye away from the surface of the vault, and each rib has its own slender respond shaft on the nave piers, visually uniting the seemingly lightweight vault with the arcade.

Sexpartite vaulting

In sexpartite, or six-part, vaulting each bay of the vault is divided into six sections by the intersecting ribs, as in the late 12th-century nave of Canterbury Cathedral, England; in contrast, the aisles have quadripartite vaults with each bay divided into four parts. Quadripartite vaults were the most common early Gothic form.

Ridge rib

At Westminster Abbey in London, built c.1260, the vaults have become much more complex than those at Canterbury. The central ridge has been articulated by a ridge rib, there are ribs over the windows, and the other ribs have multiplied with additional intermediate ribs. These intermediate ribs are called tierceron ribs.

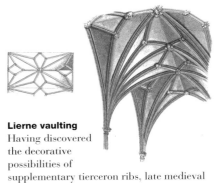

Lierne vaulting

Having discovered the decorative possibilities of supplementary tierceron ribs, late medieval architects subsequently developed lierne ribs: purely decorative ribs that connect two other ribs. Liernes have no real structural purpose, but can be used to create complex net vaults, like this one in Bristol Cathedral in England, c.1350.

Net vaulting

Although ribs are useful for adding strength to a vault, they are not strictly necessary and, by the end of the Middle Ages, vaulting ribs had become almost entirely decorative. This net vault of c.1443, which can be seen in St. Mary Redcliffe, Bristol, England, uses a cusped grid to create a rich surface pattern of elongated quatrefoils.

Rib Construction

The vault ribs are not applied to the structure, but are integral to it, and thus act to reinforce areas under strain by making them thicker. At the top of each vault compartment, a keystone or boss containing the final portion of each rib locks the whole vault together by exerting equal pressure on each part of the upper structure. Bosses are often decorated with sculpture. If properly constructed, vaults are very stable and can survive being partially ruined, but if they are not properly made and supported, they can easily collapse.

Broken vault

Vaulting can survive even if it is partially broken and ruined. The ribs and transverse arches of the ruined late 14th-century choir of Melrose Abbey, Scotland, were sufficiently strong on their own to remain stable, despite the rest of the vault having been removed. It is only the main diagonal ribs that are structural, however; the smaller intersecting lierne and tierceron ribs are merely decorative, as is the ridge rib along the top of the vault.

Tas-de-charge

The lower blocks of the vault springing, or *tas-de-charge*, incorporate all of the ribs. As the blocks progress upward, the ribs are increasingly angled until sufficient curvature has been achieved for them to be structurally stable on their own. The smaller moldings are incorporated into the larger blocks.

Vault webbing

Like the ribs, the webbing between the ribs is constructed in rows or courses laid at an angle, so that each block presses against its neighbor, rather than straight downward. In this broken vault at Sherborne Castle in Dorset, England, it is clear that even the uppermost blocks are set at an angle.

Vault responds

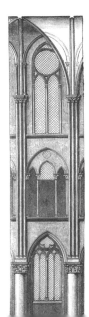

Vaulting ribs are structural, but the shafts or vaulting responds that connect the ribs to the piers below are mainly decorative. Nonetheless, long, slender vault responds, like these 13th-century examples at Notre-Dame de Paris, have a visual purpose in helping to anchor the vault onto the structure below.

Sculpted keystone

The keystone at the center of the vault is often decorated with sculpture, like this angel at Laon, France, but it also has an important structural function in locking the vault ribs together. The keystone is cut to match all the ribs, ensuring that they press against each other.

VAULTS Buttress

Vaults exert a great deal of outward pressure on the walls below them, and as a consequence require additional support in the form of buttresses. Roman and Romanesque buildings with barrel or simple groin vaults were usually reinforced with pilaster buttresses that thickened the wall at key points, but these were not strong enough to support the great weight of very high rib vaults. Flying buttresses, which utilize additional freestanding arches to reinforce the most vulnerable points of the vault, developed in the Gothic period and became a highly decorative part of the exterior of Gothic cathedrals, especially in France.

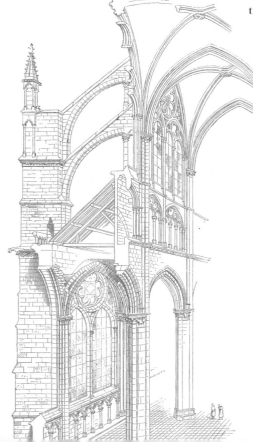

Flying buttress

The flying buttresses on the outside of the 13th-century cathedral at Amiens, France, give the building the wedding-cake appearance that is characteristic of the Gothic period. Flying buttresses support the vaults, as the arched flyers, positioned at the points of greatest stress, carry the thrust from the vaults into the mass of the buttress.

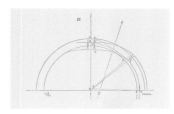

Vaulting stress points

The key stress points of a vault are the top and the haunches, where it curves over into the vertical wall. If a vault is properly constructed, the downward forces will be transmitted into the curve of the vault and into the wall; if not, it will collapse, as this diagram shows.

Arched flyers

The inherent stability of the arched flyers is used to stabilize the vaults where they exert the strongest outward force. The flyers lean inward against the vault and help to transmit some of the force down into the mass of masonry in the buttress itself.

Pinnacle

The tall pinnacles of flying buttresses add greatly to the overall decorative effect on the exterior of the building, but they also have a structural function, by adding a great weight on the top of the join between the flyer and the buttress, thus stabilizing this key area.

Pilaster buttress

Buttresses could also be used to strengthen walls that did not have vaults behind them. These pilaster buttresses are reinforcing the gable of this unvaulted English church at Manton. The buttresses are stepped, increasing in thickness toward the bottom, to give greater stability at the wall base.

Fan

The fan vault, a particularly English type, developed in the late 15th century out of the elaborate patterning of lierne and net vaults. The patterning on the fan vault carried the tracery patterns on the walls and windows up and over the vault, unifying the whole interior. Although fan vaults look impossibly delicate, they are supported by large ribs on the back, and the individual cone-shaped fans, or conoids, press against each other to lock the whole vault into position. Pendant drops add to the impression of structural impossibility, but they too are held very firmly in place by the entire underlying structure.

Blind tracery
The concentric blind tracery patterns on a fan vault, which follow the shape of the fans, continue the tracery of the windows and of the blind arcading in the lower parts of the walls. The fan vault at King's College Chapel, Cambridge, is perhaps the most famous English fan vault.

Enlarged springing

Fan vaults were initially used mainly for small spaces—such as tombs and cloisters like that at Gloucester Cathedral in England of *c.*1470—perhaps because of concerns about their structural stability. It is easy to see in this example how fan vaults developed by greatly enlarging the springing of an ordinary vault.

Fan vault construction

Whereas rib vaults put their structure on display, with a fan vault the structure is hidden on the back of the vault. As this view of the back of the Sherborne Abbey, England, nave vault shows, the fans are supported on huge ribs, which are invisible from the other side.

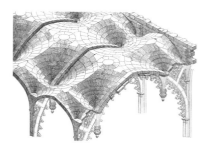

Ornamentation

A pendant fan vault gives an extremely rich stalactite-like effect. These huge pieces of masonry are partly supported on giant transverse arches, themselves covered in cusping and other ornament, creating a fantastical effect, as in the Henry VII Chapel at Westminster Abbey, London (1503–19).

Pendant vaulting

There are large structural arches on the back of the vault in the Henry VII Chapel, Westminster Abbey, London, which can be seen in this drawing. Closer inspection shows that the pendants are in fact structurally a part of these arches, despite looking as if they hang from the cone-shaped conoids on the front.

Introduction

A dome is a type of vault created by turning an arch through 360° to form a curved roof. Domes can be round, oval, or polygonal. The dome is normally expressed on the outside of the building to create a magnificent silhouette against the sky. Like vaults, domes were developed by the Romans, and were an important part of early Christian and Byzantine architecture. They were revived and developed during the Renaissance, and are a key component of neoclassical architecture. During the 20th century, architects experimented with new materials to create domes over very large spaces, such as sports arenas.

Roman dome
Domes were a common element of Roman architecture, and were also adopted by later architects who wished to invoke the Roman past. This reconstruction of the Temple of Vesta, Tivoli (1st century BCE), shows a typically shallow Roman saucer dome set on a small drum.

Early Christian domed basilica

Characteristic of early Christian and Byzantine basilicas were domes crowning the exterior massing of forms, as shown on the exterior of the church of St. Sophia, Thessaloniki, Greece (780s). The conical roofs of the lower apses are not domes, because their surfaces are flat, but help to build up the massed forms.

Renaissance dome

Domes are one of the key characteristics of Renaissance and baroque churches. They were usually placed over the central crossing space, and were often combined with a Classical temple front, as here in Andrea Palladio's Il Redentore, Venice (1577–92). The effect is majestic, with a solidity that contrasts with Gothic architecture.

Domed silhouette

Notice how a dome creates a magnificent effect against the sky, as well as allowing the creation of a very large central rotunda at the heart of the building, as shown by the US Capitol in Washington, DC. The interior is lit by a lantern and by rows of clerestory windows that are hidden behind the columns on the drum of the dome.

Continuously curved roof

London's Millennium Dome, which was built in 1999 for the 2000 millennium celebrations, has the largest continuously curved roof in the world. Made of Teflon-coated fiberglass fabric, it is not technically a dome because it has internal supports, but the exterior shape makes clear reference to Roman saucer domes.

DOMES Construction

The earliest domes were placed over round or polygonal buildings so that the dome was essentially an upward and inward extension of the wall. During the Byzantine period builders discovered that they could use triangular projections called pendentives to fill the spaces between a curved dome and a square building. Roman, early Christian, and Byzantine domes were normally constructed as a single shell of concrete or brick, but during the Renaissance, architects discovered that they could create a double-shelled dome. This enabled them to make the outside of the dome much larger and more prominent.

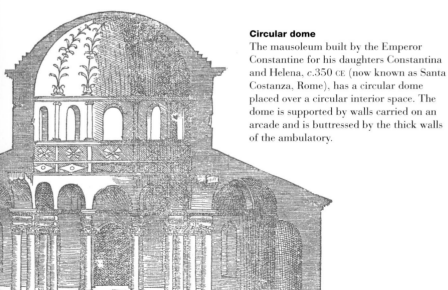

Circular dome
The mausoleum built by the Emperor Constantine for his daughters Constantina and Helena, *c.*350 CE (now known as Santa Costanza, Rome), has a circular dome placed over a circular interior space. The dome is supported by walls carried on an arcade and is buttressed by the thick walls of the ambulatory.

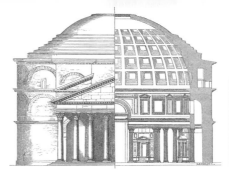

Single-shelled dome

Observe the way that in a single-shelled dome, the interior and exterior profile of the dome are closely related to each other, as this cutaway of the Pantheon in Rome shows. Although the dome is hemispherical inside, the thickness of the shell means that the outside is a much flatter saucer shape.

Pendentives

Byzantine builders made the discovery that they could use curving triangles to bridge the gaps between the corners of a square building and a round dome. These triangles, known as pendentives, made it possible to use domes over the center of a basilica, such as that of the Hagia Sophia, Constantinople (Istanbul).

Squinch

A squinch is a less sophisticated version of the pendentive, but performs the same function in bridging the gap between a square space and a polygonal or round dome. Instead of the pendentive's smooth curve, a squinch is composed of corbels or small arches.

Drum and dome

Domes need not be set directly on the roof, but can be raised above the roofs of the church by a tall, straight drum, creating a stilted effect as at the church of Les Invalides, Paris (c.1680–1720). The drum provides additional height and space for clerestory windows to light the interior.

Simple

All domes share the characteristic of being continuously curved surfaces, both in plan (horizontally) and in section (vertically), and the simplest domes are formed by turning an arch around a circle. Within these parameters, the curved surfaces can be arranged in a number of different ways. Like the arches on which they are based, domes can be round, pointed, or ogee-shaped, but the curve can be truncated vertically before it is complete to form a segmental or saucer dome, it can be raised up on a straight drum to make a stilted dome, or it can be distorted in plan to form an oval dome.

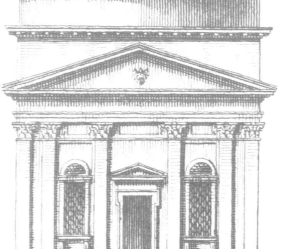

Saucer dome

A flattish dome that is like an upturned saucer, without any ornament on the top, was a common type of Roman dome. The form was popular for its historical connotations in both the Renaissance and the neoclassical period, as here on S. Andrea in Via Flaminia, Rome (1550–53), which was partly based on the ancient Roman Pantheon.

Hemispherical dome

A perfect hemisphere can be raised up on a very tall drum to give it additional height, without compromising the geometry of the form, as at Leon Battista Alberti's S. Andrea in Mantua, Italy (begun 1470). The cupola on the very top replicates the form of the dome but on a smaller scale.

Stilted dome

In contrast to a dome raised on a drum, a stilted dome, such as this one on the 15th-century Sultan Barquq Mosque in Cairo, Egypt, has straight sides that seamlessly continue the curve of the dome. This gives the dome a tall, elegant shape, but the clerestory windows at the bottom are necessarily smaller.

Oval dome

Oval domes were popular in the baroque period and made the dome an essential part of the complex, flowing masses that are characteristic of the period. The huge oval dome of the Karlskirche, Vienna (1715–37), stands over an oval nave; on the outside the form is echoed in the oval oculi windows.

Triple-shelled dome

In designing St. Paul's Cathedral in London, Sir Christopher Wren used a triple-shelled dome to create well-proportioned exterior and interior shapes without causing undue structural stress. The timber-and-lead domed roof and the lantern are supported internally on a brick cone, which is hidden behind a smaller dome.

Complex

As well as the simple shapes that are created by rotating an arch, more complex domed shapes can be made by dividing the dome's surface into sections, often with a rib or prominent curve to emphasize the division, giving the dome a more sophisticated profile. It is also possible to add extra subdomes or semidomes around the sides, an arrangement that has a structural benefit, because the curved shape of the subdome can act as a buttress for the main dome. Domes that are formed from very complex curves, such as sharply pointed ogees, are used to create the onion domes that are typical of Russian architecture.

Polygonal dome

The first polygonal dome to be built, replacing an older wooden dome, was the octagonal dome of Florence Cathedral, designed by Filippo Brunelleschi in 1419–36. An engineering marvel, it is made entirely of brick and has no buttresses other than the polygonal exedrae (domed recesses). The lantern, added in 1461, is also polygonal.

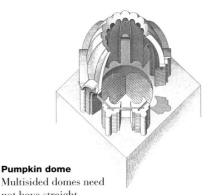

Pointed dome

Domes are a popular feature of Islamic architecture, especially for mosques, and come in many shapes, most notably the slightly in-turned bulbous form seen here at the Taj Mahal, Agra, India (1632–54). Islamic domes generally have a pointed top, rather than the lantern or cupola used on Western, Christian domes.

Pumpkin dome

Multisided domes need not have straight facets. The church of SS. Sergius and Bacchus (527–36) in Constantinople (now Istanbul) has a pumpkin dome, composed of 16 segments, convex on the outside and concave on the inside. The curving form is echoed in the window arches and the columnar buttresses.

Onion dome

Onion domes, named after their resemblance to the vegetable, have a pronounced ogee shape and are characteristic of Russian and Eastern Orthodox Christian architecture. Unlike other domes they are not normally expressed on the inside of the building, but are mainly used as external decoration.

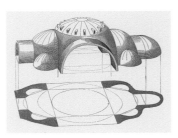

Semidome

An arrangement of semidomes exploits the strength inherent in the dome's arched form to act as both buttress and useful space. The Hagia Sophia (533–37) in Constantinople (now Istanbul) makes use of a shallow central saucer dome, flanked by exedrae (recesses) with semidomes, which are in turn supported by their own smaller semidomes.

Cupola & Lantern

Most domes are topped by a lantern or cupola—a small towerlike structure that finishes the dome and provides openings for windows and air. Cupolas and lanterns perform similar functions, but you can recognize a cupola by its small domed top, whereas a lantern usually has a pointed roof. Cupolas and lanterns can also be used on their own to ornament a roof, or to top a tower. The lantern, or lantern tower, is also sometimes the central tower of a church, where its large windows serve the same function of bringing light into the center of the building.

Polygonal lantern

The faceted surfaces of the octagonal lantern at the apex of the 15th-century dome of Florence Cathedral make its shape, which echoes that of the main dome, more pronounced. The scrolls on the small buttresses aid the transition between the curving dome and the straight-sided lantern, with a ball-and-cross finial bringing it all together.

Octagonal lantern

The octagonal central lantern tower of Ely Cathedral in England was built in the 14th century to replace the Romanesque crossing tower, which had collapsed. Made of timber painted to resemble stone, the lantern has huge windows that flood the center of the cathedral with light.

Bay-window cupola

Cupolas can be used on their own without a dome. At the Renaissance Château of Chambord in France, for instance, which was begun in 1519, the conical roofs of the large bay windows are topped by cupolas, and there is another small cupola over the central stair tower.

Neoclassical cupola

A cupola enclosed by a balustrade is characteristic of 18th- and early 19th-century neoclassical architecture. This English example is from an 18th-century house in Amesbury, Wiltshire, but this feature was also very popular in the United States and elsewhere, providing top light for stairwells or entrance halls.

Cupola ornamentation

Both cupolas and lanterns are often terminated with an ornament, such as a cross, a weathervane, or simply a decorative finial, giving a satisfying vertical finish to the whole. The ogee-shaped cupola of St. Paul's Church in Covent Garden, London, had a swan weathervane on a tall spike.

Introduction

Broadly speaking, a tower is any building that is significantly taller than it is wide. Towers, thrusting skyward, draw attention to themselves, conveying an impression of strength, power, and wealth, and are thus associated with defensive structures like castles, with religious buildings, and with civic pride. Towers are practical, because their height makes them easily defensible, and they can be used either to save space at ground level or to spread sound over a wide distance. Medieval cities and villages were punctuated by church spires, and in the modern world skyscraper towers dominate urban skylines and embody the vigor of city life.

Church tower
The Spanish city of Santiago de Compostela was one of the most important pilgrimage sites during the Middle Ages, and the spires of its cathedral and other churches were clearly visible high above the surrounding buildings, beckoning pilgrims as they approached from many miles away.

Minaret
Tall, slender towers known as minarets are characteristic features of an Islamic mosque, and minarets are often used in pairs, as here at the Blue Mosque (or Sultan Ahmed Mosque) in Istanbul. The platform at the top is used by the imam to call the faithful to prayer.

Battlemented tower
The late 14th-century Château Mehun-sur-Yèvre in France (pictured here in a reconstruction) appears very ornate, but was a defensive structure with a tall towered gatehouse, a moat crossed by a narrow bridge, thick walls with no windows in their lower parts, and battlemented towers.

Diminishing stages
The horizontal sections of a tower are called stages and may be equal in width from top to bottom, or, as in this Renaissance tower, may diminish in size toward the top. The individual stages of this tower are ornamented with Classically inspired colonnades, but these have little structural function.

Metal-framed
The Eiffel Tower in Paris was built in 1889, and at just under 1,000 feet was the tallest structure in the world. It demonstrated that metal framing could support a very tall structure, although other technological improvements, such as the development of elevators, were required for tall, enclosed buildings.

Defensive

Towers were, and still are, an important part of defensive structures, because they provide height for lookouts and enable defenders to fire down on attackers. Towers were traditionally constructed with very thick walls and small windows, making them difficult to attack, although such measures became less effective after the invention of large-caliber artillery shells. Defended towers may be built on their own, attached to a wall in the form of turrets, or as part of a larger castle complex. Aristocratic house builders also played on the castle form, adopting towers as status symbols to adorn otherwise entirely undefended manor houses.

Fortress tower

It is easy to see the importance of towers for defense on the 15th-century Spanish castle of Medina del Campo. Both the gate towers and the smaller projecting turrets on the walls enabled defenders to shoot easily at attackers, while the tall keep provided a good lookout and thick, defensible walls.

Central keep
A castle is not just a tower; it also includes thick walls, a gatehouse, turrets, and other such defenses; however, the tall central keep that stands at its center is emblematic of the castle. It was the final resort in a battle and displayed the owner's wealth and power, as here at the keep of the Old Louvre in Paris.

Tower house
Tower houses combined domestic and defensive purposes, with thick walls and small windows, but no defended outer walls. The 14th-century Langley Castle lies on the Scottish/English border, where cross-border raids were common, and would have sheltered local villagers as well as its aristocratic owners.

Irish round tower
Tall, slender, freestanding towers were one of the most distinctive features of Irish medieval architecture. Usually entered by means of a ladder through a high-level door, they were associated with monastic sites and were most probably used as temporary refuges in times of strife.

Chivalric style
The different functions of the floors in the tower of the Knights' Hall at Malbork Castle, Poland, are discernible from the sizes and styles of the windows. In particular, the great hall at the top has much larger and more elaborate tracery windows than the lower, service floors.

Church

Towers are particularly characteristic of Christian churches, and their upward-thrusting silhouettes made the church the most prominent building in a city or village. Communities competed with each other to adorn their churches with larger and finer towers than those possessed by their neighbors. The most common location for towers was over the central crossing where the nave and transepts intersected, or at the west end, but in Germany and the Low Countries especially, towers at the corners of the building were also common. Towers are typical of the Romanesque and Gothic periods, but were also used for neoclassical and Gothic Revival churches.

Crossing tower

The central crossing, where nave, transepts, and choir intersect, is the heart of the church and was often expressed externally by a crossing tower, such as that at Saint-Ouen, Rouen, France (begun 1318). It has large windows that let light into what would otherwise have been a dark interior space.

Decorated tower

A pair of western towers was a characteristic feature of large Romanesque and Gothic churches. In contrast to the plain lower facade, the tops of the 12th-century west towers of Holy Trinity, Caen, France, are embellished with bands of blind arcading, which are also repeated on the small turrets flanking the spires.

Armpit tower

Numerous small towers, including towers placed in the "armpits" of the building between the transepts and choir, are a key feature of German Romanesque churches, such as the one like at Laach, seen here. They give it an almost military appearance that complements the severity of the unornamented blind arcading.

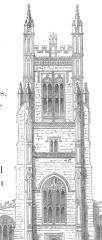

Parish church tower

The tower of a parish or village church was a symbol of local pride. Unlike cathedrals and abbeys, which often had more than one tower, most parish churches had only a single tower, which was located either over the central crossing or at the west end, as here at the English church of St. Neot's, Cambridgeshire.

Asymmetrical tower

Asymmetrical towers are characteristic of the Gothic Revival as architects sought to make buildings look as if they had evolved over time. The tower of this 19th-century church in Scotland is placed asymmetrically at one corner, giving the building a deliberately irregular silhouette.

Belfry

Bell ringing is an important part of Christian religious celebration; bells are used at weddings and funerals and on holidays such as Easter. The bells were normally hung on a wooden frame placed high up in a tower so that the sound would carry better across long distances, and the bell chamber, where the bells were located, had unglazed windows to let the sound out. Bells could also be used for civic purposes—to warn people of danger and to mark the time—and therefore many cities built tall bell towers on their town halls or civic buildings.

Freestanding tower
Collapsing towers were one of the main causes of structural failure in churches, largely because of the vibrations from ringing the bells. Where builders were unsure of the underlying foundations, they built detached bell towers, a concern that was clearly justified in Pisa, Italy, where the 12th-century tower beside the cathedral leans at an alarming angle.

Campanile

In Italy bell towers are called *campanili* (singular: *campanile*) and are usually detached from the church. The *campanile* of S. Apollinare in Classe (532–49) is one of the earliest examples of a circular *campanile* built of brick, and has round-headed windows that multiply in number toward the top of the tower.

Bellcote

Not every church could afford to have a tower for its bell, and so the bell was sometimes hung in a small bellcote over the gable. Usually made in the form of an arch set within a gable, bellcotes generally held just one or two bells.

Bell window

It is very easy to recognize the windows of the bell chamber of a tower because these windows have no glass, thus allowing the sound to escape easily. Louvers were, however, often used to keep the birds out, as here at the English church of King's Sutton, Northamptonshire.

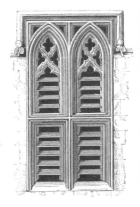

Civic belfry

Bells were used for civic as well as religious purposes, such as marking the hours and alerting people to danger. Very tall civic bell towers, like the belfry at Bruges, were common in late medieval Belgium and Flanders, and 19th-century imitations include London's Big Ben and the Philadelphia Town Hall.

Spire & Steeple

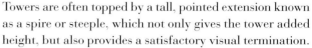

Towers are often topped by a tall, pointed extension known as a spire or steeple, which not only gives the tower added height, but also provides a satisfactory visual termination. Some writers suggest that a steeple diminishes in stages whereas a spire has an uninterrupted slope, but other writers use the term "steeple" as an alternative for "tower" and call any pointed top a spire. In practice, however, the terms are largely interchangeable. Spires can be made of stone or built of wood covered in lead, or another roofing material such as shingles. They come in a range of different shapes, including conical, pyramidal, and polygonal.

Phased construction

Spires were expensive to build and so they were often added one at a time. At Chartres Cathedral in France, the south (right) spire is late 12th-century while that on the north is early 16th-century. The south spire is lead-covered wood, but the north spire has an added stone base, reflecting greater confidence in building techniques.

Needle spire

Very tall, slender spires, often called needle spires, are characteristic of English Gothic churches and cathedrals. They are usually built of wood and covered in lead. The 14th-century example at Salisbury Cathedral, shown here, was increased in height by being placed atop a tall stone tower over the crossing.

Flèche

The very slender, spiky spire that often adorns the center of a French Gothic church is known as a *flèche*, from the French word for "arrow." Often made of iron or wood and covered in lead, a *flèche* is lighter than a traditional spire. In contrast to English churches, which combine a spire with a central tower, a *flèche* is usually built without an underlying tower.

Rococo steeple

Sinuous curves on a spire are typically rococo and often reinterpret Classical motifs, such as the shell bracket, in a more fluid way. The spire on the Austrian town church of Graz (*c.*1780) has a clock and shuttered openings, allowing sound out of the bell chamber.

Neoclassical steeple

Spires continued to be popular in the neoclassical period, and were ornamented with Classically inspired details like columns, obelisks, and urns. Books of English designs from the 18th century inspired later American builders such as Ithiel Town, who designed the Center Church in New Haven, Connecticut, in 1812–14.

Turret & Pinnacle

A turret is a small tower, usually placed at the corner of a building. Like larger towers, turrets project above the roofline, but they are generally too little to contain more than a small staircase. Pinnacles are even smaller than turrets, and are normally only decorative, with no internal space at all. Pinnacles are often used on the tops of buttresses, where as well as being decorative, they provide an important downward pressure.

Both turrets and pinnacles are characteristic of the Gothic period, and are an important aspect of the late medieval trend toward micro-architecture: the use of miniaturized architectural motifs as decorative elements on a building.

Pinnacle

Pinnacles on buttresses not only help to create a very delicate silhouette characteristic of late Gothic architecture, but also help to weight the buttresses against the outward thrust of the vaults, as here on the late 14th-century church of St. Barbara, Kutna Hora, in Bohemia (the modern Czech Republic).

Corner turret

The small size of turrets makes them less dominant than full-scale towers in the same position, yet they still provide strong visual terminations. Along with the smaller pinnacles above each buttress, the four corner turrets of King's College Chapel in Cambridge, England (1446–1515) are a distinctive feature of its exterior profile.

Tower pinnacle

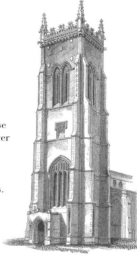

Pinnacles were often used to decorate the corners of Gothic towers, as on this English church in Cromer, Norfolk. The pinnacles served to soften the otherwise sharp edge of the tower top, and they also reinforced the tower by providing extra weight on the corners.

Stair turret

You can easily recognize stair turrets by their many small windows, as is clear from the stair turret of the Bishop's Palace in Salisbury, England. The octagonal shape of the turret and the diagonal placement of the upper windows reveal the curve of the spiral stair within.

Tourelle

Small turrets set high on the corner of a wall are characteristic of the Scottish baronial style (seen here at Balmoral Castle) and of the French Gothic châteaux on which it was based. Known as *tourelles* or pepper-pot turrets, they are usually round and have conical roofs.

153

City

Towers have been a fundamental part of city architecture for many centuries, because their multiple levels are an ideal way of creating additional floor space without taking up room at ground level. Towers have been used as a way of displaying civic pride, and private owners have also built towers to display their personal wealth. More recently, company wealth and power have been displayed through ever-larger skyscrapers. Tower building in confined urban areas brings its own special problems, for towers need both to be visible above other buildings and to make an impact at ground level.

Art Deco spire
The Chrysler Building (1928–30) in New York plays with the architectural vocabulary of a Gothic tower, including gargoyles, parapet, and spire, but adapts it to the Art Deco style. The concentric arches with their chevron pattern draw the eye upward and ease the transition between the square building and the tapering spire.

Renaissance civic tower

Italian Renaissance merchants competed to build very tall towers on their town houses, and such towers were also built on city buildings like the Palazzo Publico (Town Hall) in Siena, seen here. The battlements make reference to defense, but were mainly for show, because the building below was not defensible.

Gothic Revival town hall

The enormous central tower of Manchester Town Hall, designed in 1887 by Alfred Waterhouse, still dominates the city center and acts as a permanent reminder of Manchester's status as one of England's main commercial centers. Based on late medieval town halls in the Low Countries, it is designed in a Gothic Revival style.

Early skyscraper

The American Surety Building was built in 1894–96 in New York for a bond insurance firm. Its towering form and innovative construction features were meant to convey the strength and security of the company, while the prominent cornice, elegant rustication, and columnar lower stories meant that it stood out visually.

Modernist tower

The Seagram Building in New York was designed in 1957 by Ludwig Mies van der Rohe with Philip Johnson. Its sheer glass sides and unadorned mass made it hugely influential on later skyscraper design.

Introduction

A door can lead us into a building or deliberately deny us entrance. The placement and type of doors can be indicative of the building's use. The main door is one of the most important parts of a building and is often heavily ornamented. Styles of doorways changed markedly over the centuries and they can therefore be a good tool by which to date a building. Secondary doors indicate their subsidiary function through smaller size and less elaborate decoration. Doors are frequently further emphasized by steps, and sometimes by a porch, which keeps off the rain and draws attention to the door itself.

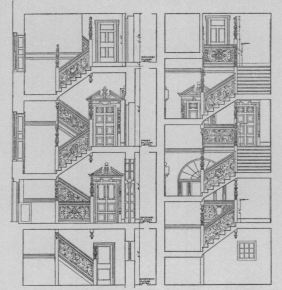

Hierarchy of doors
The door often says something about the room it closes, and different-style doors are used to indicate a hierarchy of rooms. In the 17th-century Cromwell House at Highgate in London, the doors are different on each floor, with those at the top (perhaps into servants' rooms) being considerably simpler.

Portcullis

The entrance to a castle is frequently protected by a portcullis—a large metal-and-wood gate that was dropped in front of the entrance from above. As well as the portcullis, here there is also a pit in front of the entrance, which could be covered by a removable drawbridge.

Graded doors

The number and placement of doors can offer clues to the arrangement of the building behind. Here, on the west facade of S. Maria in Cosmedin, Rome, there are three doors; the larger central one leads into the nave while the smaller side doors lead into the side aisles.

Amplified entrance

In designing the entrance to St. Saviour's, Venice, the 16th-century architect Andrea Palladio emphasized the doorway by making the column spacing of the portico subtly wider in the center. The side doors so common in the Gothic period are here represented only by niches with statues.

Narthex

In early Christian churches, such as the 4th-century basilica of (Old) St. Peter's in Rome, the entrance was through a porch, or *narthex*. The *narthex* was used by the catechumens (believers who had not yet been baptized), while the church itself was reserved for the faithful.

Greek & Roman

The door was not a conspicuous feature of either Greek or Roman buildings because it normally stood behind a large portico, but it was still emphasized with a certain amount of ornament. The usual form of a door opening had inward-tapering sides, probably as a result of the need to give the stone lintel added support at its ends, although doorways became straighter-sided during the Roman period as builders became more confident. The opening was encircled by a molded surround, often ornamented with motifs such as rosettes, and was topped by a projecting cornice supported on console brackets.

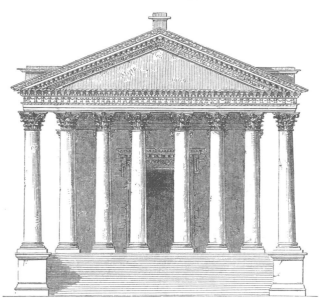

Partially hidden doorway
In both Greek and Roman temples, much of the worship took place not inside the building but on the steps outside. As a consequence, the door into the inner chamber, or *cella*, was almost hidden behind the columns of the portico, as here at the Temple of Bacchus at Baalbek in Lebanon.

Etruscan doorway

The Etruscans lived near Rome in the 8th–4th centuries BCE. The most characteristic feature of Etruscan architecture is the doorway with sharply tapering sides and an overhanging lintel, sometimes represented, as here in an Etruscan tomb at Castel d'Asso, by a carved surround. It probably derived from Egyptian models.

Tower door

The door to the Tower of the Winds in Athens (1st century BCE) has a pediment that is supported on a pair of fluted columns with modified Corinthian capitals. The inner opening is still angled, but this angle is almost entirely disguised by the surround.

Double doors

This reconstruction of the Erechtheum, situated on the north side of the Acropolis in Athens, shows it with a pair of large double doors. The surround is a simple band of rosettes, but this is topped by a more elaborate projecting cornice supported on a pair of console brackets, and the sides of the frame tilt inward slightly.

Arched doorway

The entrance into the early Christian (5th century CE) church at Turmanin, Syria, borrows the form of the Roman triumphal arch, with a central arched opening flanked by two smaller arches. Inside the porch, or *narthex*, the actual door has a molded surround with a heavy cornice.

Portico

A portico is a covered walkway in front of or around a building. It may also have a gable above it. The concept of surrounding a building with a covered space that is open on one or more sides is extremely ancient and is common to most hot countries. The porticoes of Greek and Roman temples were very precisely defined according to the number of columns and their placement, whether in front of the building, between two projecting walls, or purely as a symbolic portico attached to the facade. The same rules for creating porticoes were also adopted in the neoclassical period.

Hexastyle

Common portico arrangements include octastyle (eight columns), hexastyle (six columns), and tetrastyle (four columns). The even number of columns creates an odd number of openings, allowing an opening directly into a central door. The portico of the Greek Revival church of St. Pancras, London (1819–22), is hexastyle.

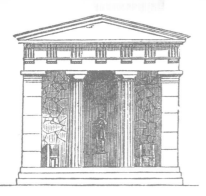

In antis

A portico *in antis* is enclosed between two short projecting wall stubs (*antae*), which end in square projecting pilasters that finish off the portico. This portico at the small temple at Rhamnus in Greece is distyle, with only two columns, but more could be used.

Peristyle

A colonnade that entirely encloses the building within, behind a screen of freestanding columns, is called a peristyle. The peristyle of the Hephaesteum in Athens is peripteral because it has a single row of columns; a double row of columns is called dipteral.

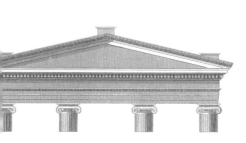

Pediment

The pediment is a key element of the portico. Supported on an entablature above the portico columns, it represents the gable end of the pitched roof ornamented with a molding on all three sides. Pedimented porticoes were often used on their own in later periods as a large-scale ornament.

Engaged portico

Along the sides of the 1st-century CE Roman Maison Carrée in Nîmes, France, the columns are fixed to the sides of the inner *cella* building, creating a so-called engaged portico. Those at the front, however, project beyond the building, creating a prostyle (projecting) portico there.

Romanesque

Romanesque church builders placed great emphasis on doorways. The shape of the door usually followed the prevailing fashion for round arches, and the surround was heavily decorated with layers of ornament. The head of the arch might be filled by a central tympanum that provided a field for sculpture, and the building's thick walls enabled the side jambs to be angled inward and embellished with layer upon layer of ornament. The internal division of the building into a central nave with side aisles might be clearly expressed by multiple doors. The central door was generally reserved for grand processions, with the side doors being used on more ordinary occasions.

Recessed door
The plainness of the facade of the 11th-century church of S. Pablo in Barcelona only serves to highlight the heavily decorated door. The area around the door has been thickened, enabling the doorway itself to be deeply recessed, and there is a sculpted tympanum over the opening.

Projecting doorway

The late 11th-century doorway of the church of Saint-Trophime in Arles, France, has a surround that projects to become a shallow porch. Probably an adaptation of a Roman portico, it has a gabled top and the arch is supported by a sculpted frieze like an entablature, which rests on dwarf columns.

Sculpted doorway

Every part of the main west doors of the Spanish cathedral of Santiago de Compostela is covered in sculpture, including the central tympanum representing Christ in Glory and its supporting trumeau pillar. The door jambs have columns sculpted as figures, and there are also figures around the *roussoirs* of the arch.

Order

The term "order" is used to refer to an arched molding supported on columns in the Romanesque and Gothic periods. This door from Heilsbronn near Nuremberg in Germany has four orders, the outermost of which has a thick cable or rope molding. The door itself has a trefoil head.

Tympanum

The head of the arch over this early 12th-century English doorway has a tympanum panel with a sculpted image of Christ flanked by angels. The sculpture on the jambs is less clear and may represent Adam and Eve on one side and a hunting scene on the other.

Gothic

Overall, the basic arrangement of doors and doorways in the Gothic period changed relatively little from the preceding Romanesque period. Prominent west portals, usually arranged in threes—one each for the nave and side aisles—remained a key feature of larger churches. Doors in the Gothic period followed the prevailing styles and shapes, notably in terms of using the pointed arch shape, and in adopting currently fashionable forms of decoration such as finely detailed moldings, crockets, and foliage capitals. The doors themselves were also ornamented, especially during the late Gothic period, when they became fields for decorative carving such as blind tracery panels.

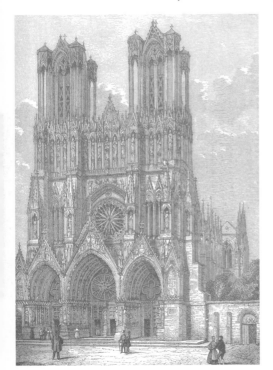

Triple portal

A triple portal with three doors, one for each of the nave and two side aisles, is a key element of Gothic cathedral design, as here at Reims, France. The portal itself projects, permitting many layers of ornament, and each opening is further emphasized by a crocketed gable.

Porch

This Gothic parish church porch would have protected worshippers from the rain as they entered the building, but would also have served as a useful space in and of itself. Church porches were used for the first part of the wedding service, for making contracts, and as schoolrooms.

Hood molding

The square molding over the top of this 15th-century English doorway is called a hood mold or a drip mold. A common late medieval feature, its ends have "head stops" with faces. The doorway itself has a four-centered head that is set within a square frame.

Banded brick doorway

As with many other aspects of architecture, the nature of the door surround partly depends on the materials being used. This late Gothic brick house has a relatively simple doorway made from layers of banded light and dark brick, but no sculpture, as this is difficult to achieve in brick.

Blind tracery paneling

It was not only the door surround that was ornamented in the Gothic period. The door itself was also frequently decorated. This blind tracery panel comes from a door in the convent of Blaubeuren in Germany, and utilizes typical late medieval motifs consisting of rectilinear panels, cusping, and sinuous ogee curves.

Renaissance

The Renaissance revival of forms from Classical Antiquity, and especially from ancient Rome, had an important impact on the design of doors, as Classical forms were introduced in place of the preceding Gothic style. Facades based on temple fronts became popular, and rectangular door frames with continuous architraves were again common, as were doors topped with cornices supported on brackets. Doors themselves were decorated with Roman-influenced motifs such as coffering. Arched doors continued to be used, but the arches were now rounded in the Roman manner and often had prominent keystones. In northern Europe, doorways were very elaborate.

Triumphal arch
Renaissance architects reacted against the perceived excesses of the Gothic. Motifs such as giant pilasters, triumphal arches, and heavy pediments were revived and applied to the facades of churches and palaces. The central triumphal arch and huge, flanking pilasters of S. Andrea, Mantua, Italy (begun 1470), dwarf the doors into insignificance.

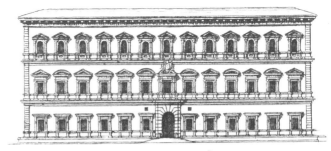

Coffered double doors

This door, leading into the Palazzo Rucellai in Florence, has a rectangular frame with a decorated architrave and prominent cornice, which are closely derived from ancient models, as are the coffered double doors. The facade itself is articulated with pilasters: Doric at ground level and Corinthian above.

Rusticated doorway

The 16th-century Palazzo Farnese in Rome has a simple, massive doorway ornamented only with prominent rustication on the *voussoirs* (wedge-shaped stones) around the opening. Such openings were not direct copies of ancient forms, but were developed in the Renaissance as architects were inspired by the past.

Inventive ornament

The entrance to the Town Hall at Leiden in the Netherlands, built in 1595, is typical of northern European Renaissance architecture.
Standard Italian motifs, like the entablature carried on columns, round arches, and niches, are used, but they are decorated with inventive ornament based on French models that owe little to Classical precedents.

Strapwork detail

The entrance to Blickling Hall, Norfolk, England (1612–27), has a tall, projecting porch with bay windows at either side. The complex strapwork detailing is influenced by the architecture of the Low Countries. At the sides are Italian-influenced loggias, which still make use of northern detailing.

Baroque & Rococo

Along with windows, doors were one of the most important decorative aspects of baroque and rococo architecture. The most common aspect of door decoration in this period was a pediment. This could be rounded or pointed, and could have additional elaboration with a so-called broken (or divided) base or apex, often itself ornamented with sculpture. New types of door surrounds, notably the banded surround with prominent alternating blocks of masonry, also became more popular during this period. In the interior decoration of the rococo period, doors lost some of their prominence, becoming only one aspect of an overall decorative scheme that covered all interior surfaces.

Baroque doorway
The Church of the Gesù in Rome (begun 1568) was an early example of a baroque design that was widely copied later. The three doors, one each for the nave and side aisles, are treated as only one element of a complex two-storied facade using curved and pointed pediments and two levels of pilasters.

Blocked surround

Blocked columns, which have every other block made larger and square, were a common baroque device to add interest and variety to an opening. Here, blocked columns are used on a doorway that also has a prominent keystone that is "dropped" below the edge of the opening.

Broken pediment

Broken pediments enabled architectural variety and elaboration. Here, an interior door surround from the Banqueting House in London, designed by Inigo Jones (1573–1652), has an eared architrave. Above that there is a broken-apex pediment supported on brackets, with a female bust in the center of the pediment.

Atlantes

Late baroque and rococo doors combined a wide variety of ornamental details to create lavish entrances, like this one into a projecting porch. Atlantes support the balcony over the porch, and are joined by other mythological figures, paneled double doors linked by a fanlight, and a variety of shells and drapery.

Eared architrave and panels

At Cromwell House in London, a broken pediment with a central finial gives a rich finish to the mid-17th-century door. The eight panels diminish in size toward the top. The uppermost panels and the architrave have ears, and there is strapwork on the architrave.

Neoclassical

The key aspect of neoclassical door design was the use of a pedimented porch, either in the form of a full-scale portico or as a smaller and simpler porch over the door alone. Complete with columns, these porches often made use of elaborate modillion cornices and other bold ornament. Neoclassical doors were usually paneled, with a six-paneled arrangement being the most common, and were often surrounded with glazed openings, including fanlights above the door and sidelights next to it.

Interiors also made use of paneled doors, but these often had complex decoration in plaster and other delicate materials.

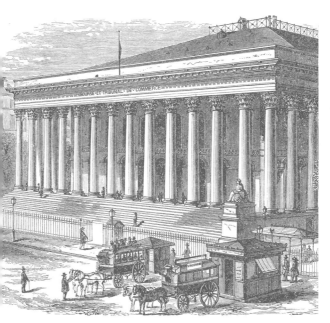

Corinthian portico
As well as recalling the glories of the ancient world, an enormous portico gives a building a sense of grandeur and monumentality in a crowded urban setting. The early 19th-century Bourse in Paris has a Corinthian portico across its full width. The actual entrance doors are hidden behind the portico.

Fanlight

An arched window over a door is called a transom light or fanlight, a name relating to the radiating design often used in such windows. This French neoclassical example has a central roundel under an arched head and elaborate ironwork, but simpler radiating designs were also common.

Delicate detailing

Interior decoration was often much more elaborate than external decoration, because delicate details survive better under cover. This interior neoclassical door has an eared architrave surmounted by a frieze with a central medallion bust and seated caryatids at the sides, which in turn supports a cornice bearing Greek key, or meander, design.

Pedimented porch

This porch takes the form of a portico and reduces it to a smaller scale, with attached columns at the side to link it visually to the house, and steps up from ground level. Its details include Corinthian columns and a heavy modillion cornice. The door itself is six-paneled.

Sidelights

Narrow windows at the sides of a door opening are called sidelights. Here, in the 1814 Hunt-Morgan House, Lexington, Kentucky, they are combined with a fanlight.

The arrangement is related to a Palladian opening, but the fanlight is in fact wider than the arched upper section of a Palladian window.

19th Century

Like other aspects of 19th-century architecture, doors were designed in a wide variety of revival styles and were often a key component in evoking the desired style. Gothic Revival styles were particularly popular for doors and porches, because it was easy to use an arched opening or some stained glass to evoke the Gothic Revival; but Classical detailing was also used. New building types such as apartment buildings, warehouses, and factories required new forms of doorways that were large enough to provide access for vehicles as well as people, and that could give sufficient grandeur to a large building.

Gothic Revival porch
With its open sides set on low stone walls, the porch of this half-timbered cottage is a key component of its Gothic Revival style, although it is actually based on the model of a church porch. The entrance itself has a four-centered opening that would have been mirrored by the actual door that it covers.

Porte-cochère

A *porte-cochère* is one of the most distinctive features of French apartment buildings. Very large doors provide access for vehicles into a covered passageway, with doors on either side leading into the residential areas. The term is also used for a large outdoor porch through which a carriage or other vehicle may drive.

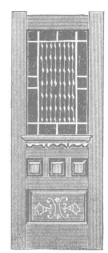

Part-glazed door

Part-glazed doors, with the upper part of glass and the lower part of wood, were very popular in the late 19th and early 20th centuries. They were used both as front doors and as internal doors to share the available light between rooms. This example has etched glass, but stained glass was also frequently used.

Integral porch

Here the doors into adjacent late Victorian terraced houses in London are set back under integral porches, which enable the doors to be opened out of the rain without extending the front line of the house. The two porches are unified with a single depressed arch on early Gothic-style pilasters.

Art Nouveau doorway

This Parisian doorway, designed by the French Art Nouveau architect Hector Guimard (1867–1942), exploits the structural possibilities of cast iron and glass to create an extremely graceful and sinuous design. It was only with the development of structural metals that such large areas of glass became possible.

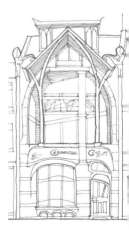

Modern

The constructional similarity of Greek trabeated (post-and-lintel) construction and curtain-wall construction, which also uses interlocking uprights and horizontals, meant that classical porticoes were a major inspiration for 20th-century architects. Much as had been the case in the ancient world, continuous colonnades were used to unify the entrances into very large buildings. The introduction of curtain-wall building techniques and the improved manufacturing of plate glass also enabled the construction of fully glazed fronts, including wholly glazed doors, creating the curious effect of being able to see into the building while making it difficult to see how to open the door.

Fully glazed front
The Peter Jones department store in London was one of the first buildings to have a fully glazed front supported by a huge steel beam. This enabled the construction not only of continuously glazed windows, but also of glass doors to tempt potential shoppers into the building.

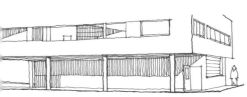

Colonnaded facade

It is very difficult to see how to enter the Villa Savoye, near Paris, designed by the Modernist architect Le Corbusier in 1928, because it was designed not for pedestrians but for vehicles, which can drive up a special ramped entrance behind the columns that support the house.

Tuscan porch

The porch of this early 20th-century suburban house was intended as an outdoor living space. It has Tuscan columns, which were common on porches, partly because of their associations with Italian Renaissance loggias and partly because they were simple and cheap to make.

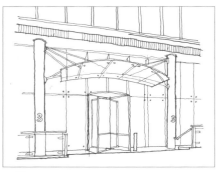

Glass canopy

Here a glass canopy projecting over the entrance is used to articulate the facade of an entirely glass-fronted office building in London. A glazed revolving door, with hinged doors at the sides for fire access, provides both visual and physical access to the interior offices.

Unified facade

The structural supports for the facade of the Lincoln Center concert hall in New York create an entrance colonnade that draws inspiration from ancient Greek models. Much like a classical colonnade, it has the advantage of providing multiple access points while creating a fully unified facade.

Introduction

The English word "window" comes from the Old Norse for "wind eye," and windows are one of the most important features of a building, not only letting in light and air, but also—like eyes—giving a building much of its character. Window styles have changed greatly over time, and recognizing the different styles can be a good way of dating a building. This section provides an overview of the key developments. But beware, for windows can be changed. Windows are one of the easiest features of a building to replace, and throughout history people have updated buildings in this way.

Updated
Mismatched styles can be a clue to changes. For example, the lower windows in the English tower of St. John the Baptist, Devizes, Wiltshire, have Gothic Perpendicular–style tracery inside and heavy Romanesque ornament around the outside, suggesting that the tracery was added later to update the windows.

Sash

Sash windows are characteristic of 18th- and 19th-century English and American architecture, and were probably invented by the English scientist Robert Hooke (1635–1703). The panels of glass slide vertically over each other, and individual sashes may be divided into smaller panes by wooden muntins, or glazing bars.

Casement

Casement windows were common during the Gothic and Renaissance periods. They remain popular in Europe today, and are widely used in Modern buildings. Casements can be hinged at the sides, at the top or bottom, or even in the middle. These casement windows have outward-opening panels like small glazed doors.

Closers

A window in a stone or brick building is usually edged with a line of alternating short and long stones or bricks, as in this Romanesque window. If the glass pane is removed and the window is blocked up, these "closers" often remain, giving clues to the window's former presence.

Dormer

Dormer windows, which project outward from a building's roof under small roofs of their own, can be used to provide additional living space in the roof, without adding to the overall height. This 18th-century American dormer has a Palladian sash window, but casements were also commonly used.

Greek & Roman

Like the buildings they are part of, Greek and Roman windows are generally constructed using a trabeated (post-and-lintel) system to create a rectangular opening. The surrounds are typically angled inward to support the lintel better and provide an attractive shape. Some Classical buildings, such as temples, had few windows, but were decorated with niches instead. These could contain statues and were usually topped by a small pediment.

Windowless building

Most Greek and Roman temples, including the Maison Carrée in Nîmes, seen here, did not have any windows in the *cella*, or central shrine room. During the neoclassical period, adapting the temple form to buildings with windows was to prove problematic for architects.

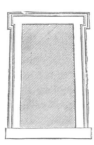

Vitruvian

Windows that are narrower at the top than at the bottom and have very simple surrounds with small, projecting ears at the top corners, as at the Erechtheum in Athens, are called Vitruvian windows. They became an important feature of neoclassical architecture.

Tivoli

This window from the Temple of Vesta at Tivoli in Rome (*c*.80 BCE), is similar to the windows of the Erechtheum, but has ears at the bottom as well as at the top. Revived by Andrea Palladio, this was an important shape in the Renaissance, baroque, and neoclassical periods.

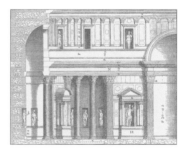

Niche

Instead of, or in addition to, windows, many Roman buildings had similarly shaped niches to hold statues, or merely as decoration. The niches in the Pantheon in Rome have alternating triangular and curved pediments on the lower level and simple cornices in the upper story.

Improved lighting

Christianity placed great emphasis on the faithful being able to see during services, and so early Christian churches were better lit than older temples had been. Old St. Peter's in Rome had windows in the apse, aisle windows, and high-level clerestory windows to bring light into the central nave.

Romanesque

Romanesque windows were generally constructed using round arches, producing a rounded head to the window. Concerns about the structure meant that most Romanesque windows were small and were used either singly or in small groups. In the early Gothic period, as pointed arches were developed and builders became more confident about the structural properties of stone construction, larger and taller windows were created. These early Gothic windows were tall, thin lancets, but soon came to be used in groups and in varying sizes and shapes, pointing the way toward the development of more elaborate windows with tracery during the 13th century.

Widely spaced, round-headed windows

A typical Romanesque elevation, with widely spaced, round-headed windows without tracery, appears here, on the late 12th-century Worms Cathedral, Germany. The transepts have a more decorative group of three windows, but these, too, are generously spaced so as not to compromise the stability of the unbuttressed wall.

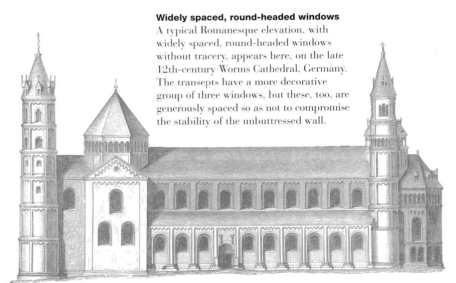

Chevron ornament

This English window from St. Cross in Winchester is given added interest on the inside by a pair of small colonnettes and a band of chevron ornament around the head of the window. The window itself is deeply splayed in order to let in more light from the small opening.

Lancet

This tall, thin window with a sharply pointed head and no internal divisions is known as a lancet, after the medical instrument it resembles. Lancets are characteristic of early Gothic architecture of the late 12th and early 13th centuries before the development of tracery.

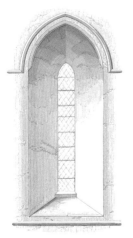

Splayed window

The inner edges of a window opening can be angled, or splayed, to let more light into the building. Splayed windows were most popular during the Romanesque and the early Gothic period when windows were still small. The splay can also be angled to direct the light to a particular part of the building.

Stepped lancets

The middle window of this early 13th-century group of three trefoil-headed lancets is placed higher than the others, creating a stepped arrangement. Stepped lancets, which also occur in fives, represent an important early stage toward the development of tracery by greatly reducing the amount of stone between the openings.

Gothic

The windows of the Gothic period are characterized by pointed arches, stained glass, and tracery. Plate tracery, where the openings seem punched through the wall surface, developed in the early 13th century, but builders soon realized that intersecting arches and curves could be used to create more open bar-tracery patterns. Early tracery used geometric shapes like arches, circles, and trefoils, but the 14th-century introduction of the reverse-S ogee led to the development of much more complex and sinuous patterns. The stone tracery patterns were complemented by the use of decorative stained glass.

Bar-tracery rose window

This rose (round) window has bar tracery, which replaced plate tracery during the mid-13th century and enabled the development of very elaborate patterns. Instead of the window being treated as a solid surface with glazed openings, the glass predominates and the stone has been reduced to curving bars amidst the glass.

Plate tracery

A plate-tracery window appears to have shaped openings punched through the wall. This plate-tracery rose (round) window from Chartres Cathedral in France has a multifoiled circle surrounded by quatrefoils above two lancets. The overall effect is of many separate windows placed together in an attractive arrangement.

Reticulated tracery

The sinuous in-and-out ogee curves in the head of this English window from the Friary in Reading create an interlocking netlike pattern that gives such tracery its name of net, or reticulated tracery. Reticulated tracery was particularly popular during the 14th century.

Stained glass

Stained-glass windows, like this 13th-century example from Auxerre, France, are made up of small pieces of different-colored glass that are held together by strips of lead called "cames." They are characteristic of the Gothic period, and commonly depict miracle stories, figures of saints, and geometric patterns.

Lucarne window

In the Gothic period, spires were often decorated with small dormer windows, known as lucarne windows, as can be seen in this English example from Wilby, Northamptonshire, of c.1400. Lucarnes are mainly decorative, but they also helped to ventilate the interior of the spire and to provide light for any interior repairs.

Late Gothic

During the late Gothic period, tracery patterns were very elaborate, with complex, flowing ogee curves. In England especially, ogee tracery in the head, or top, of the window was often combined with intersecting vertical mullions and horizontal transoms to create a paneled effect. The Renaissance had begun in Italy during the 15th century, but the Gothic style persisted in northern Europe into the 16th century. Newer Renaissance motifs crept in, however, and were mixed with older Gothic forms, creating a style that was neither wholly Gothic nor fully Renaissance and that included simpler Renaissance-influenced tracery patterns with little or no elaboration.

Flamboyant tracery

During the later Gothic period, ogee curves were used to create complex flowing patterns like these that are in a window from St. Mary's, Dinan, France, of *c.*1450. Characterized especially by a teardrop-shaped pattern, "flamboyant" (as in flames), "curvilinear," and "flowing" are all names given to such tracery.

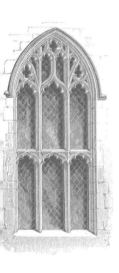

Perpendicular tracery
English late Gothic architecture is known as the Perpendicular style, a name it gains in large part from the characteristic paneled effect that was created, as here, by the use of vertical mullions and horizontal transoms set perpendicular to each other.

Hood molding
This early 16th-century English window has a square head enclosing two rows of four-centered openings that are separated by a transom. Around the outside of the window is a hood molding: a raised, three-sided band, usually with decorative ends, which helps to divert the rain away from the glass.

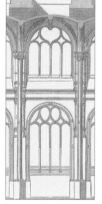

Uncusped tracery
The early Renaissance in northern Europe saw a stripping down of older forms and the reintroduction of older motifs such as the round arch. In Saint-Eustache, Paris (begun 1532), the round-headed windows have uncusped lights, and the ogees create strong, flowing curves without the elaboration of earlier periods.

Mixed Renaissance and Gothic
Gothic and Renaissance forms are used together in this early 16th-century window in the church of Saint-Laurent, Nogent-sur-Seine, France. The overall appearance of the window retains a lingering sense of the Gothic, as do the tall mullions, but the surround displays Renaissance-influenced decorative motifs.

Renaissance

In Italy, early Renaissance windows were often biforate (twin-opening), with two round-headed openings within a larger opening, a form that actually owes much to earlier Gothic forms. Increasingly, however, forms derived from ancient Rome came to dominate, including pediments, cornices, and Classical columns and pilasters. Windows in the form of Roman arches set within an entablature were also popular. As the Renaissance progressed, windows increasingly became rectangular and were topped by pediments: small decorative gables that are placed over the opening. In northern Europe, mullions and transoms continued to be popular, but there, too, rectangular shapes and pediments proliferated.

Alternating pedimented
A combination of tall rectangular windows topped by pediments and rounded niches, also with pediments, creates interest and variety at the east end of St. Peter's in Rome. The clerestory windows are horizontal rectangles and feature cornices on ornamental brackets.

Arched

The late 15th-century Scuola Grande di San Marco in Venice has windows in the form of Roman arches. They are set within an architectural frame that comprises pilasters carrying an entablature surmounted by a pediment. Combined with round-headed niches and rounded gables, there is little of the Gothic left here.

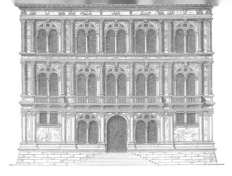

Biforate

This early 16th-century Venetian palace has biforate (twin-opening) windows with a large round arch subdivided into two round-headed lights topped by a roundel. Also known as a Venetian arch, this shape was very fashionable in both Italian and northern European architecture during this period.

Mullion and transom

By the late 16th century, windows were typically rectangular and divided into many panes by means of intersecting vertical mullions and horizontal transoms. English Renaissance great houses like Longleat, Wiltshire (1570s), often had numerous large windows to display the owner's wealth.

Bay

Tall bay windows, which punctuate the facade and echo adjacent towers, were typical of Renaissance palaces and great houses. The 16th- and 17th-century castle of Fredricksborg, Denmark, has curved bay windows on its gable-end walls and square bays on the main facade.

Baroque & Rococo

Baroque windows, as with other aspects of baroque architecture, built on the foundations of the Renaissance, but were made much more elaborate, with variations in shape, notably the use of curves. Pediments were the dominant motif of baroque windows, with new types and forms of pediment being developed, including broken-apex and broken-base forms. During the late baroque and rococo periods, pediments often became extremely elaborate. New window shapes, such as the oval *oeil-de-boeuf* (bull's eye), were also developed, as were new types of surrounds, including those utilizing rustication, banded masonry, and giant keystones.

Baroque combinations

The variety and inventiveness that are characteristic of the late baroque period are seen here in the windows of the Kollegienkirche in Salzburg, Austria. The main apse and tower windows have a mix of rounded heads with prominent keystones and complex pediments, and there are oval windows in the clerestories of the nave and dome.

Broken-base pediment

This window head from the 16th-century Hôtel de Vogüé in Dijon, France, has a broken-base pediment, where the lower part of the pediment is divided. Here it is further elaborated with a female bust between garlands, giving a rich and elaborate effect.

Oeil-de-boeuf

Oval or round windows were popular in the baroque period, and are commonly called *oeil-de-boeuf*, or bull's-eye, windows. Often enclosed in an ornate surround, they were most often used for gables, dormers, and roofs, where the unusual shape provided added visual interest in the upper part of the building.

Dropped keystone

This window has three oversized keystones whose lower edges hang below the upper edge of the surround, an arrangement called a "dropped keystone." A common baroque feature, they provide added emphasis to the window head and are used here with a surround of prominently rusticated blocks.

French window

French windows are full-length casements that open all the way to floor level, enabling one to walk through them like doors onto a terrace or balcony. Derived from French Renaissance and baroque buildings such as the Place Royale in Paris, they are now widely used for more ordinary houses.

Palladian

The work of the 16th-century Italian Renaissance architect Andrea Palladio was extremely influential during the 18th century through publications of his work, and nowhere was this more evident than in the design of windows. Window styles first widely used by Palladio in his designs came to be key motifs of 18th- and 19th-century neoclassical architecture. The Palladian window, which bears his name, has a central round-arched opening flanked by two smaller, rectangular openings whose entablatures support the central arch. Palladio also made use of the so-called Diocletian window, a semicircular opening that was popular for high-level structures like gables and clerestories.

Multiple Palladian forms

The early 18th-century Burlington House in London makes use of all the main Palladian and neoclassical window forms: the lower story has rusticated surrounds with prominent dropped keystones; the sides have Palladian windows; and there are alternating pointed and rounded pediments in the middle.

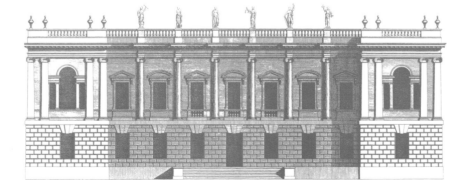

Palladian window

Popularized by Andrea Palladio, the Palladian window, also known as a Venetian window or Serliana, was extremely popular in the neoclassical period. It has a central round-arched opening that is flanked by a pair of smaller straight lights with columns and entablatures. Doors can also be made in this way.

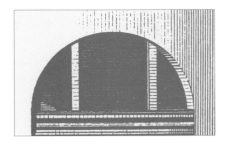

Diocletian window

A semicircular window, that is usually divided (as here) into three compartments by two vertical mullions, is known as a Diocletian or thermal window. Derived from the early 4th-century Baths (*thermae*) of Diocletian in Rome, it was commonly used in neoclassical buildings for gable windows and other high-level openings.

Palladian influence

Palladio's designs were very influential on the design of ordinary houses in the 18th century, leading to the Georgian (English) and Colonial (American) style. Not only were his rectangular box plans and hipped roofs popular, but Palladian windows—used here on the ground floor—and pediments were also common.

Rusticated surround

The windows of this early 18th-century London house are set within rusticated arcades. On the lower story is a simple arcade, while the upper story has an additional frame of an entablature with pilasters. The openings themselves would have had sash windows, although they are not shown here.

Neoclassical

The late 18th- and early 19th-century neoclassical period saw the introduction of Greek forms in place of the Roman-inspired forms that had dominated the Renaissance, baroque, and Palladian periods. In particular, the portico and continuous colonnade were key forms, but this led to a problem: Greek temples did not have windows, and architects therefore struggled to find ways to marry the portico with the need for natural light in the interior. In terms of actual window forms, the rectangular sash window was the most common, and was frequently made in different sizes in order to create pleasing visual proportions on the facade.

Glazed colonnade
Friedrich Schinkel's Schauspielhaus (theater) in Berlin, of 1818–21, shows how this great architect coped with the demands of combining the usually windowless classical temple form with a building that needed many windows. He did this by creating what are essentially glazed colonnades along the sides of the building.

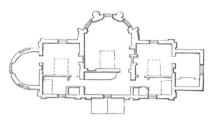

Sash window

The demolished Apthorpe House in New York City (built 1762) had rectangular sash windows topped by pediments on the main floor, and smaller, square sashes above and in the dormers. Window sizes were related to the nature and location of the rooms, with those at the top of the house being smaller.

Bow window

Curved bay windows are usually called bow windows, and give a graceful and elegant exterior profile. Bow windows were especially popular during the late 18th and early 19th centuries, and were sometimes mirrored inside by another curve to create an oval room.

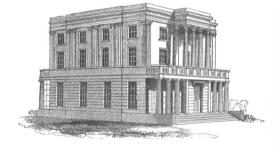

Neoclassical motifs

This house in Salem, Massachusetts, of *c.*1800, was influenced by the Scottish 18th-century architect Robert Adam and uses typical neoclassical motifs. The lower windows are set within a blind arcade, while those above are framed within pilasters. The small, square windows on the top floor are typical of the period.

Neoclassical villa

The neoclassical temple-style shell of this early 19th-century English villa is just that, for the sash windows give away its real function as a house. Architects often found it best to confine the portico to the front, because this made it easier to provide good interior light.

Victorian

The Victorian period was dominated by a series of revival styles, and by a number of mixed styles that incorporated aspects from many different periods. The main type of window remained the sash window, but it could take on different shapes, such as a pointed arch, to indicate the Gothic Revival, or different patterns of glazing bars to denote the Queen Anne style. Bay windows were especially popular, with canted, or angled, bays being the most common form in the mid-19th century, and flatter, square bays becoming more common in the late 19th and early 20th centuries, although canted bays continued in use.

Terraced bay window
Bay windows were very popular for terraces, or rows of urban houses, because they increased the amount of light in a confined area without taking up too much additional space. They also gave potentially long and dull street facades a much more pleasing rhythm.

Gothic sash window

During the Gothic Revival period, Gothic-style sash windows were made. These examples have a variety of pointed and ogee-shaped heads and hood molds combined with traditional sliding sashes. Such windows gave a house a stylistic flavor without the need to change fundamentally the method of construction.

Queen Anne bay window

Windows with geometric patterns of small square and rectangular lights, usually in the upper part, were a key decorative component of the so-called Queen Anne style. Popular in the late 19th century, this was entirely unrelated to the style of the real, early 18th-century English Queen Anne.

Outside blind

Frames like these, which look like exterior wooden pelmets or valances, are sometimes seen above the windows on 18th- or 19th-century houses. As well as being decorative, they held the fittings for exterior canvas sun shades or blinds, which were highly fashionable during this period.

Full-pane sash window

Each sash of these windows has a single pane of glass, undivided by glazing bars, an arrangement common from the mid-19th century onward and still much used today. These large expanses of glass were made possible by improvements in glass-making technology that enabled the production of larger sheets of glass.

Commercial

The modern store window, with its vast expanse of glass, is a fairly recent invention. There were stores in the ancient world, and the Greeks even had shopping centers called *stoas*, but these were more like market stalls with lockup areas behind. During the Middle Ages, purpose-built stores closed with wooden shutters became common in towns and cities. Improvements in glass-making techniques during the 18th century led to the development of glazed store fronts, and during the later 19th and 20th centuries the introduction of plate glass and of curtain-wall techniques enabled the construction of fully glazed store windows.

Medieval store window
In the Middle Ages, store windows were not glazed, but rather, as in this late medieval French example, were closed with shutters, which could be opened to form an awning above and a counter below. At night the shutters were closed and locked, providing good protection against thieves.

Bow-fronted store window

This curved, or bow-fronted, store window in London is a rare survival of a once-common 18th-century type made possible by improved glass-making techniques. It has curved panes of glass held in place by muntins, or glazing bars. Below the window is a solid wooden section called the "stall riser".

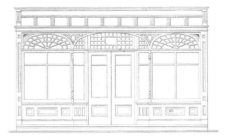

Queen Anne store front

This typical late 19th-century store front has a central door. There is a solid stall riser at the bottom, large plate-glass display windows, and a decorative Queen Anne–style section at the top, which is high enough not to interfere with the view of the goods being displayed.

Divided display window

The very large ground-floor windows of the Egyptian Halls in Glasgow, Scotland (1873) were made possible by the use of cast iron in the structure of the facade, although the glazing itself was still supported in timber frames and there were structural posts between the individual bays of the display windows.

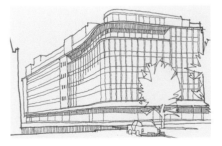

Undivided display window

The display windows of the Peter Jones department store in London (1932–36) are fully glazed without any intermediate structural dividers. This was made possible by the use of an enormous steel beam above the display windows, one of the earliest examples of its type.

Modern

Modernist architecture of the 20th century was characterized by a lack of ornamentation. Modern windows are commonly just simple glazed openings without any detailing around the frame, and they are frequently used in a variety of sizes to create a satisfying appearance without superfluous ornament. The availability of large sheets of plate glass, and the development of structural technologies including long-span steel beams and curtain-wall construction, enabled the creation of very large, undivided windows and fully glazed exterior walls. Nonetheless, in smaller buildings such as houses, older styles like sash windows remained popular long after they had gone out of fashion in larger buildings.

Pattern of voids
Even though these windows at Highpoint, London, of 1935, have no ornament, they form a pattern of voids against the solidity of the wall surface—an arrangement typical of Modernist architecture. The accompanying balconies are an important part of this effect, as is the variation in size between the large picture windows and the smaller casements.

Ribbon window

Windows like these, which are considerably longer than they are high, are called ribbon windows. They were made possible by new construction techniques in the 20th century, such as the use of large steel beams that were able to support heavy loads without intermediate vertical supports.

Suburban oriel window

An oriel window is a small bay window that projects from the wall above ground level, as here. Common during the Gothic period, oriel windows were revived during the late 19th and 20th centuries. On this 1930s house, an oriel window is used in conjunction with sash windows.

Curtain-wall glazing

Buildings that look as if they were made of glass are one of the most characteristic features of the 20th century. This illustration of the famous Bauhaus architecture school in Dessau, Germany, shows how it is done, with an inner structure and an outer curtain wall of glass that forms the windows.

Sealed window

Modern technology plays an important part in the design of later 20th-century windows, as in the Seagram Building, New York. The glass window walls of many modern buildings do not open, making the occupants dependent on air conditioning. Although visually striking, this is ecologically problematic because it uses up far more energy than simply opening the windows.

Introduction

At a basic level, stairs are simply about getting us from one level to another in a building, but in reality stairs have a much more fundamental place in the design of buildings. They can add drama and grandeur to both inside and outside; they can invite us to come in, or make it difficult for us to gain access to other levels. The design of staircases has changed over time, making them a good dating tool, and looking at the position and nature of a staircase can help to give us an understanding of how a building was intended to be used.

Podium
A stepped podium gave added grandeur to a Greek temple such as this 6th/5th-century BCE example from Paestum in Italy, and also provided a firm platform for the columns to stand on. The uppermost step, upon which the columns rested, was known as the stylobate.

Spiral stair

Spiral, or newel, stairs, set around a central newel, or pillar, were the most common type of stair during the Middle Ages, and could be made from wood or, as seen here, from stone. They were particularly popular for castles because their confined space and limited views made them easily defensible.

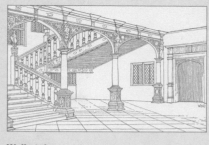

Well stair

During the Renaissance period, spiral stairs became less common and were replaced by well stairs, like this example from Knole House, Kent, England, of c.1605, which goes up in short, straight flights around an open well. The newel posts at the corners are often heavily decorated.

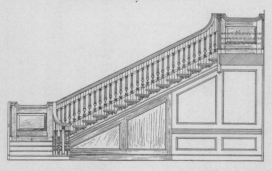

Entrance stair

Here, a broad flight of steps is used to add a sense of drama to the entrance of the Redentore Church in Venice, begun in 1577 and designed by Andrea Palladio. The pilasters create the sense that the stairs narrow inward as they approach the door, drawing the worshipper inside.

Straight run

During the neoclassical and Victorian periods, long, straight flights of stairs were fashionable, as were elegant sweeping curves, especially for the handrail. This 18th-century example has a long, straight flight, and the handrail makes a graceful curve around the newel post at the bottom.

Construction

A staircase differs from a ladder in having depth as well as height, which is important because the depth makes a staircase easier to climb than a ladder. Not only is it possible to put your foot fully on each step, but a forward and upward motion is easier than going straight up. The parts of a staircase are all related to making it simple to climb. The basic components are the horizontal treads and the vertical risers; these are held in place by "strings" along the sides, while balusters support the handrail and keep us from falling off the stairs.

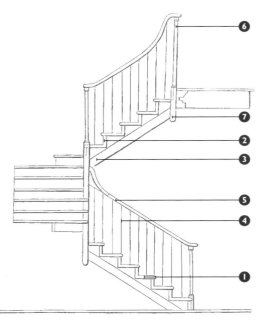

Parts of a staircase
This diagram shows the key parts of a staircase, including the treads (1), risers (2), and the string (3) along the sides. There are also balusters (4), a handrail (5), and newel posts (6). The upper and middle newels are further decorated on the underside with a pendant drop (7).

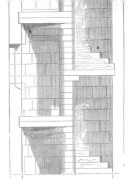

Spiral-stair construction

This cutaway view of a spiral staircase shows how the treads are arranged. Each step is cut from a single block of stone, the ends of which are stacked to create the central newel. The weight of the newel holds one end of the step, while the other end is bedded into the wall.

Alternating treads

The number of treads controls the height of a staircase. When space is very tight and a steeper stair is required, the treads may be made in an alternating pattern, as here. This creates twice as many treads in the same height, but is more difficult to walk up.

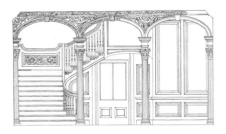

Open-string stair

It is possible to see the ends of the treads and the sides of the risers in this stair, giving this very common type of staircase the name "open-string stair." In contrast, a closed-string stair has a diagonal board covering the ends of the treads and risers.

Well stair

A well stair rises around a central opening, or well, as shown here. The stairs go up in short flights and make right-angle turns at each landing. The newel posts act as the main supports, and the stair is also firmly attached to the wall.

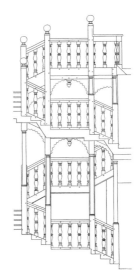

Medieval

Stairs were an important part of the design of medieval castles and churches. In churches, the altar was usually raised on a stepped platform, adding drama to the liturgy and making the altar more easily visible from the back of the church. Spiral stairs, which were curved around a central newel post, were the most common type of stair used for access between floors in castles and great houses. In castles they were often designed in such a way as to make it more difficult for attackers to reach the upper stories. Smaller houses may have had ladders for access, but these rarely survive.

Stepped altar platform
The altar of a medieval church was usually raised up on top of a platform approached by a short, broad flight of stairs, as seen in this example in Ravenna, Italy. The stairs set the altar apart from the rest of the church as a special area, and draw attention to it even when no services are being celebrated.

Exterior stair

Anyone climbing this external stair leading up to the raised entrance of the Romanesque-period Castle Rising, Norfolk, England, would have been horribly exposed to defenders looking down from above. During more peaceful times, the stair added drama and grandeur to the entrance.

Stair turret

Spiral staircases were usually set into a curved compartment or stair turret. Such turrets have a distinctive pattern of windows following the shape of the stair upward, as here at the Bishop's Palace in Salisbury, England. The stepped effect of the windows clearly shows the shape of the stair.

Palace stair

Not all spiral stairs were used for purely defensive purposes. This grand example from a late medieval French palace has an ornate ceiling, large stained-glass windows, and is wide enough for several people to ascend together. The door on the left leads to a smaller service stair.

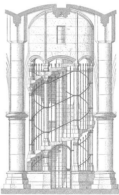

Freestanding spiral stair

Spiral stairs require some form of support for the outer ends of the treads, but this need not be a solid wall, as this splendid French Gothic example shows. Here the stair is surrounded by a curving colonnade of small shafts on a curving string that holds the treads.

Renaissance

During the Renaissance, stairs became grander and more complex. The reliance on spiral stairs gave way to a variety of new designs, including elaborate double helixes, well stairs that had straight flights turning around a central well, and curved stairs. The presence of a well, or opening, at the center of the stair required the use of a handrail, and balusters to support it. Balusters were often turned, with complex mirror-image patterns being particularly popular, but a variety of other designs were also used, including ones that were based on contemporary forms of ornament, such as strapwork. Newel posts were also heavily ornamented at this time.

Double-helix stair

The main staircase in the French Renaissance Château de Chambord takes the form of a double helix, with two separate sets of spiraling stairs—a reflection of the Renaissance fascination with complex designs. It is possible to go up one flight without meeting someone coming down the other flight.

Twin external stairs

The Italian Renaissance Palace of Caprarola, near Rome, has two great external staircases, one curved and the other straight-flighted. These add drama to the entrance of the palace and exploit the visual drama of the steep slope on which it is set.

Decorated well stair

Like other architectural elements, staircase decoration followed the fashions of the day. This 17th-century well stair from Cromwell House in Highgate, London, has strapwork panels decorated with trophies. The newels have standing figures in contemporary dress, and there are prominent pendant drops on the undersides of the corners.

Turned balusters

Characteristically in this period, balusters were quite thick, and the upper and lower sections were often mirror images of each other. These late 16th-century balusters were turned on a lathe. The handrail is broad and flat, and the newel posts have prominent finials.

Splat balusters

So-called splat balusters, which are carved from flat planks of wood rather than being turned, were another characteristic type of Renaissance baluster. These English examples are symmetrical from side to side, but not from top to bottom, and have a tapering shape with a cutwork open area at the center.

Baroque & Rococo

Like other aspects of baroque design, baroque staircases borrowed heavily from the Classical design repertoire, but added enough variety to create elaboration without being fussy. Tapering vase-shaped balusters were particularly popular in the baroque period, but in the 18th century much more elaborate designs—including spiral shapes and balusters made to look like miniature columns—were also used. New materials (notably cast iron, which became more widely available in this period) were utilized to good effect to create delicate designs that were not possible in wood; and open-string staircases, in which the ends of the treads and risers were exposed, were also introduced.

Vase-shaped balusters

The graceful vase-shaped balusters of the 17th-century Ashburnham House in London, designed by Inigo Jones, were influential in introducing much simpler, Classically inspired baluster forms into England. The overall effect, including the simple square newel posts and flat handrails, is derived from Italian Renaissance and baroque balustrades.

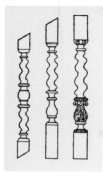

Twisted balusters

Twisted or spiral balusters were popular in the early 18th century and became a distinctive feature of stairs of this period. They were turned on a lathe and usually took the form of an open corkscrew spiral, although tighter spiral shapes can also be seen on some examples.

Mixed balusters

In the middle of the 18th century staircases with mixed balusters—including twisted and spiral shapes, as well as miniature columns complete with capitals and bases—were popular. There was no standard pattern or combination of balusters, but many such staircases repeated the same combination of three on each tread.

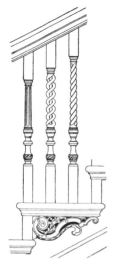

Ironwork panel

Late 17th- and 18th-century improvements in metal-working techniques made cast-iron balusters popular. Light and strong, they could be made in delicate patterns. Initially very expensive, they were used for high-profile projects like Hampton Court Palace in England, as seen here, but in later years they became more widely available.

Rococo balusters

The asymmetrical C-curve characteristic of the rococo period lent itself to staircase design along with other decorative elements. These cast-iron balusters use C-curves to bridge the height gap between treads, creating a more continuous line up the stair. Notice that the treads now have an open string.

Neoclassical

In Palladian and neoclassical architecture, staircase designs drew heavily on ancient models. The temple facade, complete with stepped podium, was a key element of buildings of this period and could be used either as the main element of the facade or as one part of a larger design. As rows of terraced houses became more widespread, new uses for stairs, such as the split stair combining access to the raised front door and the sunken service area, were developed. Inside, staircases were simplified, with straight flights, sometimes combined with a gentle curve, becoming more common. Balusters, too, took on new shapes based on antique models.

Stepped podium
Thomas Jefferson's design for his house at Monticello, Virginia, has a projecting portico raised up on a stepped podium that draws heavily on Greek models. Jefferson deliberately chose what he perceived to be the more democratic Greek style over the Roman style, which was considered to have royal or imperial connotations.

Exterior stair

Lord Burlington's Chiswick House in London, begun in 1725, was strongly influenced by Palladian models. The elaborate multiflighted external staircase on the entrance front, seen here, is based on the stairs of Renaissance Roman villas, but is combined with a temple portico based on antique Roman models.

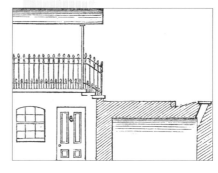

Area

Short flights of steps descending into a lower-ground-floor space called an "area" are common in neoclassical town houses, and usually, as here, open onto a door at the bottom. They developed from the need to provide access for servants and deliveries without going through the front door.

Circular stair

Unlike a spiral stair, which has a central newel post, a circular stair curves around an open well. Circular stairs were very fashionable in the 18th and early 19th centuries, as in this mid-18th-century curving stair from a large London town house.

Adam-style balusters

Cast-iron balusters such as these, designed by the important neoclassical architect Robert Adam, have a tapering pilaster form that is topped by small Roman-style lanterns. The strength of the iron, even when it is very thin, enabled the pattern to be extremely delicate, a characteristic of Adam's work.

Revival Styles

The staircases of 19th-century revival buildings were usually based on models drawn from the period that the architect wished to evoke. Thus a Gothic Revival building would have tracery-work balusters, while a Renaissance Revival building would have a grand stair in the Renaissance manner. These evocative motifs were, however, often just that: motifs applied to a standard design that had little to do with the true form of older models. This was particularly noticeable in houses, where the stair was normally made in a standard pattern, with different details applied to the balusters and newel posts to evoke different periods and styles.

Gothic Revival stair
This early 19th-century Gothic Revival-style staircase uses two-light tracery panels in place of balusters and a closed string over the ends of the treads and risers. The use of a straight-flighted stair and a chunky newel post, however, clearly marks this as a 19th-century, not medieval, stair.

Oversized stone stairway

This stair from the 19th-century Palais de Justice in Paris is in a Renaissance style that is in keeping with the rest of the building. Made of stone, it is massive to the point of being oversized, in harmony with its prominent position at the heart of an important public building.

Service stair

Until relatively recently, many families—even middle-class ones—had servants. If possible, an additional staircase was provided so that the servants did not have to use the family staircase. In this 1870s house there are two sets of stairs, with the smaller service stairs leading directly to the kitchen.

Mass-produced balusters

The development of fully mechanized lathes enabled all kinds of turned balusters to be mass-produced during the 19th century. These balusters, from a late 19th-century builders' catalogue, show just a few of the many different kinds of designs that were available cheaply and easily to home builders.

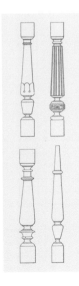

Neoclassical newel post

At their best, 19th-century designers combined elements from older styles to create designs that captured very closely the spirit of older styles, without being exact copies. This superb 1870s newel post, with its lion's head, rosette, and acanthus leaves, is derived from neoclassical models, without being a slavish copy.

Modern

In the 20th century the ever-increasing number of tall buildings placed new demands on staircases and on the technology of going up and down. Not only were fireproof stairs required for factories and offices, but there is a limit to how many flights of stairs anybody wants to climb, and so tall buildings have required new means of vertical transport, most notably the electric elevator, which was developed in the late 19th century. Escalators, or moving stairs, were developed at the same time. More conventional stairs were not forgotten, however, and architects have continued to design stairs using the latest decorative detailing.

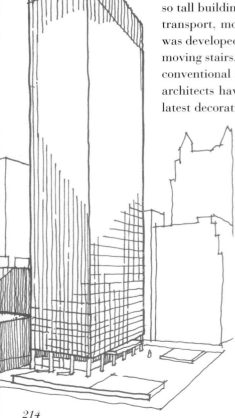

Electric elevator
Tall buildings depend on mechanized methods of transport between floors to make them feasible, because most people do not want to climb more than a certain number of flights at any one time. The introduction of the electric elevator was the key to the development of very tall skyscrapers, such as the Seagram Building in New York.

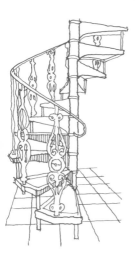

Iron spiral stair

The widespread availability and low cost of cast iron in the 19th century made freestanding cast-iron spiral stairs like these popular. Compact and easily adapted to different ceiling heights, they were widely used in factories, offices, and other commercial buildings, and were usually painted.

Art Nouveau stair

This staircase, designed by the Art Nouveau–architect Hector Guimard, uses the fluid potential of cast iron to take on shapes that are almost impossible in wood or other materials, creating a very graceful and elegant design. Nonetheless, the basic dogleg shape of the stair remains unchanged from the standard 19th-century pattern.

Escalator

Most escalators are constructed with straight runs of steps, but there are some curving examples, such as this one in a California shopping mall. Escalators in department stores and shopping centers are usually in the middle of the building to enable people to see goods as they travel between floors.

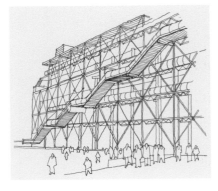

External escalator

During the late 20th century, architects looked for new ways to explore the visual potential of stairs, and other means of vertical transport. On the Pompidou Center in Paris (1971–77), designed by Richard Rogers and Renzo Piano, the escalators are housed on the outside in prominent tubes.

Introduction

The Romans had complex underfloor heating systems called hypocausts, and medieval castles and palaces had fireplaces, but it was not until the 16th century that fireplaces became widespread in smaller houses. Before that time, most houses had a single main room with an open fire at the center, which was used both for heating and for cooking. Fireplaces are constructed in such a way that smoke is directed up the chimney through a flue, and there is often a mantelpiece or shelf above to improve heat circulation. Both fireplaces and chimneys follow prevailing fashions and can be a good dating tool.

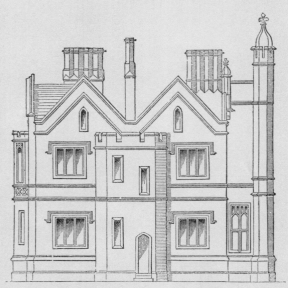

How many fireplaces?
You can usually tell how many fireplaces are inside a house from the chimneys outside. Each has its own flue that vents the smoke through the chimney, and these are normally visible at the top of the chimney. Count the flues and you count the fireplaces. On this house there are nine.

Hypocaust

As this diagram depicts, the Romans developed elaborate underfloor heating systems, or hypocausts, that were most commonly found in bathhouses, but were also used in palaces and villas. Heat from a furnace was conducted through spaces under the floor to warm the rooms above and to heat water for bathing.

Elaborate chimneystack

The heavily embellished chimneystacks of the Château de Chambord in France (begun 1519), which have a variety of decoration including roundels, chevrons, and lozenges, are typical of the Renaissance period. Fireplaces were very expensive, and elaborate chimneystacks were a way of prominently displaying the owner's wealth.

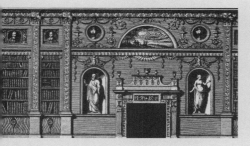

Ornate fireplace

In small houses the fireplace is often the main decorative element in a room, but in larger houses it is usually only one element in an overall design. In the Long Gallery of the neoclassical Syon House near London, the elaborate fireplace is part of a grand decorative scheme.

Cooking hearth

Until fairly recently, smaller houses had only one fireplace that was used for both cooking and warming the living space. This 19th-century French house shows how, with iron hooks for pots over the fire, ornaments and pans on the mantelpiece, the room was decorated for eating and living.

Medieval

In the Middle Ages, the main living space or great hall was heated by a central open hearth whose smoke escaped through the high roof, and great houses tended also to have separate kitchens to reduce the risk of fire. Enclosed fireplaces were restricted to the very largest and grandest buildings, such as castles, palaces, and abbeys, and even then there might be only one or two. These fireplaces were usually made in the form of a projecting smoke hood supported on columns or corbels, while the chimney itself projected from the outer face of the wall.

Open hearth

The great hall was the heart of a medieval house and had an open hearth at its center. The roof timbers were open to the ceiling, as here at the Great Hall at Sutton Courtenay in Oxfordshire, England, to enable the smoke to filter upward, and there were one or more vents called smoke louvers to let it escape.

Abbey kitchen

Medieval castles, palaces, and abbeys often had detached kitchens to keep the cooking smells away from the living spaces and to reduce the risk of fire. They frequently had more than one hearth, for cooking many dishes. This enormous fireplace comes from the kitchen at the abbey of Blanche de Mortain in Normandy, France.

Canopied fireplace

This enormous projecting canopy at the house of Jacques Coeur in Bruges, Belgium, which is supported at the front on freestanding columns, is a typical late medieval fireplace. The fire itself would have been built on the hearth below, with the canopy acting as a hood to direct the smoke up and out through the chimney behind.

Timber smoke hood

In this French medieval house a timber smoke hood is used instead of a chimney to direct the smoke upward and out of the house. Although a timber chimney may seem odd, the wood did not come into direct contact with the flame, and could therefore be used safely.

External chimneystack

Medieval chimneys were usually set against the outside face of the wall, as here, rather than being integrated into it. In part this may reflect the frequent addition of chimneys to buildings originally designed without them, but it may also result from concerns about structural stability.

Renaissance & Baroque

Improvements in brick-making techniques in the 15th and 16th centuries made chimneys more widely available, but fireplaces were still extremely expensive. The owners of houses with fireplaces drew attention to this fact through the use of very elaborate chimneystacks on the outside of the house. Ornament followed prevailing fashions, and during the Renaissance decoration derived from Classically inspired *all'antica* motifs was particularly popular. In the later baroque and rococo periods, fireplaces were decorated with the fashionable C-curves, shells, scrolls, and swags. Elaborate overmantels or chimneypieces that enabled the display of sculpture over the fireplace also became popular during this period.

Multiple chimneystacks
The multiple brick chimneystacks of the early 16th-century Compton Wynyates in Warwickshire, England, highlight the many fireplaces inside. There is a variety of designs, including spirals and lozenges. Their asymmetrical placement is partly due to the arrangement of the rooms, and partly because the building developed gradually over a period of time.

Decorative chimney

Built-in fireplaces were a great luxury even in the 15th and 16th centuries, and houses with fireplaces had elaborate chimneys to let everyone know about them. The chimneys were heavily decorated and were often different from one another. These English 16th-century chimneys from Tonbridge, Kent, are made of specially carved and shaped bricks.

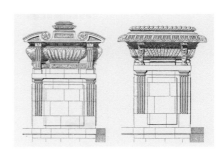

French Renaissance chimney

This elaborate pair of chimneystacks are embellished with *all'antica* motifs, are shaped like Roman sarcophagi (highly decorative stone coffins), and ornamented with pilasters, pediments, masks, and moldings, including egg-and-dart. They show how Classical motifs were adapted to new uses during the Renaissance and were employed to display wealth and power.

Ornate chimneypiece

In grand baroque rooms, the actual fireplace was only one part of a much larger sculptural composition, with a decorative chimneypiece above the fireplace. This example from the Château de Villeroi in France has a portrait bust in an oval garlanded frame, set within a larger frame and topped by a curved broken pediment.

Mirrored overmantel

This fireplace from the Palace of Versailles near Paris has a mantel shelf with elegant scrolling C-curves and shell decoration. The area over the fireplace has a mirror made to look like a window, but a real window in this position would have been impossible because of the chimney behind.

Neoclassical

Visible chimneystacks did not suit the purity of Classically inspired buildings very well, and so in the neoclassical period chimneys were often hidden, either by placing most of their length within the roof or by concealing them behind a parapet. However, this was not always easy because improvements in both fireplace and chimney designs saw fireplaces become taller and shallower, and the chimneys made longer to improve the draft. Fireplaces had flanking pilasters and a straight mantelshelf like a projecting cornice above. The sides could be plain or fluted, and in the early 19th century bull's eyes in the corners were also popular.

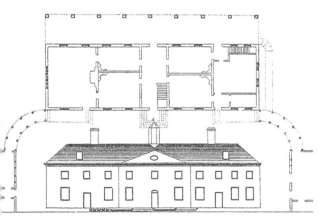

Multiple fireplaces
George Washington's house at Mount Vernon, Virginia (1757–87), has two chimneystacks, one toward each end of the house. The plan shows how these chimneys were able to serve multiple fireplaces inside, which would each have had a separate flue within the main stack, with separate flue stacks almost hidden within the hipped roof. Positioning them in this way enabled them to serve two sets of rooms.

Partially concealed chimneystack

Thomas Jefferson's unexecuted competition design for the president's house located in Washington, DC (1792) draws heavily on Palladian models, with a central dome and porticoes on all four sides. The unavoidable chimneystacks, necessary to provide heating, are largely hidden within the hipped roof, but nonetheless are still visible externally.

Adam fireplace

This fireplace in the style of the Scottish architect Robert Adam makes use of a range of neoclassical decorative motifs, including the Greek key or meander pattern. There is a projecting mantelshelf based on a cornice, and the pilasters at the sides are represented by female heads with garlands.

End stack

On this house the chimneys are located on the side, or end, walls and would have served fireplaces placed one above the other on each floor. This arrangement, called an end stack, was common in the 18th and 19th centuries and could also be adapted for terraced or row houses.

Bull's-eye fireplace

This illustration shows one of the most common types of early 19th-century fireplace. It has a roundel or bull's-eye motif in each corner. Here the sides of the surround are plain, but they could also be fluted. This design could be made in marble or in painted wood.

19th Century

Two key features can be seen in the design of 19th-century fireplaces. The first is the use of detailing derived from a range of older styles, such as Gothic Revival, as well as designs that mixed elements from many different periods, including the baroque and neoclassical. The second is changes in the design of the interior of fireplaces related to attempts to improve their efficiency, including the introduction of smaller grates specifically intended for burning coal. The range of materials used for fireplaces widened too, as cast iron, which was usually painted, was introduced. Decorative tiles were also popular.

Louis XIV-style fireplace
Styles from several different periods were popular for 19th-century fireplaces. This one is based on a mid-17th-century French style from the period of King Louis XIV and could have been carved in stone or cast in metal. It would have been part of a very richly decorated interior.

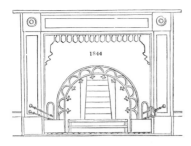

Arched insert

The design of the interior fittings of fireplaces developed in the 19th century as people looked for ways to make burning coal, the main fuel, more efficient. A small, shallow opening was found to be best, and therefore inserts like this arched cast-iron example were developed and used inside larger fireplace surrounds.

Cast-iron fireplace

This fireplace, typical of the late 19th century, is made of cast iron. It has details drawn from a range of periods, including both Classicizing elements, like egg-and-dart molding and fluted metopes, as well as delicate floral detailing. There are tiled inserts at the sides, and the small grate is designed to burn coal.

Chimneypot

Chimneypots, such as these early 19th-century examples, were a way of extending the chimney's length and hence its upward draft. This set is polygonal and raised up above the top of the actual chimney on a small plinth, but chimneypots are also commonly round. They are generally made in cast terra-cotta.

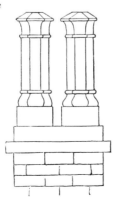

Tudor Revival fireplace

This 19th-century fireplace was copied from a 16th-century English example and might have been used in a Gothic Revival or Tudor Revival interior. A very plain four-centered arch is set within a rectangular frame. The spandrels between the arch and the frame are ornamented with elongated triangles.

20th Century

Fireplaces became ever less important in the 20th century as new methods of heating using oil, gas, and electricity were developed. Although both gas and electric "fires" were made to look like fireplaces and followed the prevailing design fashions, the increasing use of central-heating systems meant that no fireplaces at all were needed to heat Modern buildings. Concerns about pollution also reduced the use of real fires, especially coal fires. Nonetheless, people continue to enjoy having a real fireplace, and houses are often still built with fireplaces, although now they appear only in one or two main rooms, while other rooms are heated by alternative means.

New types of heating

Sometimes, what isn't there can tell you as much about a building as what *is* there. This house, which was designed in the 1930s, has only one chimney. This is not because the other rooms were unheated, but because new types of gas, electric, and oil-fired heating did not require large chimneys.

Exposed stack

The prominent exposed stone-and-brick chimney on this American house, which was probably intended as a country retreat, was made deliberately rustic to evoke the sense of a pioneer past. This type of revival remained popular for small houses long after it had gone out of fashion for larger ones.

Coal heater

Enclosed stoves and heaters were first introduced in the 18th century, and were greatly improved in the 19th century. This very elaborate early 20th-century coal-burning heater with rococo detailing had many advantages over a fireplace, not least that it had only a flue pipe and did not require a chimney.

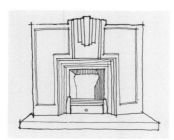

Art Deco fireplace

This Art Deco fireplace might well have been used as a surround for one of the gas and electric "fires" that became popular after World War I. This type of fireplace was often covered with tiles, usually in a plain solid color, although patterns were also very popular.

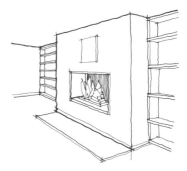

Hole-in-the-wall fireplace

The desire to sit in front of a real fire persists right up to the present day, and designers and architects have responded with new fireplace designs, such as this very plain "hole-in-the-wall" style that suits the stripped-down Modern interior of recent years.

Introduction

Ornament is a fundamental part of architecture, and is used to enliven surfaces, highlight particular parts of a structure, and generally make the building more attractive. Designers in all periods of architectural history have exploited a huge variety of motifs, ranging from human and animal forms through foliage and flowers to all manner of geometric designs. Architectural elements such as pediments and gables are also used decoratively, and even simple variations in texture can be highly ornamental. This section takes a look at the main classes of decorative ornament and helps you understand how it has been used over the centuries.

Light and shade
Subtle variations in the depth of carving can add enormously to the visual complexity of an ornamental pattern. On these blocks, rustication—the shadow pattern created by the angled grooves between the blocks—creates a far more sophisticated effect than would be possible with flatter carving.

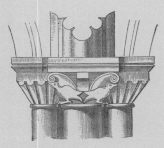

Paired motifs

Using multiples of the same motif is a common decorative device that has been employed in all periods of history. Here, two swans with intertwined necks provide a sinuous centerpiece for a Romanesque capital from Speyer, Germany, while also recalling the actual mating behavior of these long-necked creatures.

Addorsed forms

One simple way of creating interest and variety in a design is to use the same object mirrored. This is particularly common with birds and beasts, which are said to be "affronted" if they are face to face and "addorsed" when they are back to back, as here with these Romanesque birds.

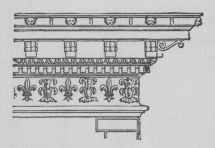

Repeated forms

Multiplication of forms creates variety without being overly elaborate. In the Romanesque cloister at Tarragona, in Spain, the arcade is carried on paired shafts with paired sets of moldings. The twin round openings above repeat the doubling motif, and give a 3-2-1 effect with the outer arch.

Alternating motifs

The alternation of motifs can keep a very regular design from looking dull. Here, on the entablature of the Palazzo Farnese, Rome, fleur-de-lys alternate with Gothic-derived foliage, thereby breaking up the design while still maintaining the symmetrical rhythm.

229

Human Figure

The human figure is one of the most fascinating decorative motifs and is common to most periods of architectural history. Human figures can personify a part of a building, such as a column; they are most frequently used in religious contexts as freestanding or relief sculptures. Partial human figures can be combined with other elements, such as animal parts, to create bizarre and grotesque figures. These grotesques were usually meant to amuse onlookers with their sheer preposterousness. Not all religious cultures welcome the depiction of the human form, however; some view it as potentially leading to image worship, and the breaking of images is known as iconoclasm.

Caryatid

A caryatid is a column personified as a female figure, who stands gracefully, easily supporting the weight of the building on her head. Common in ancient Greek architecture, and during the Greek Revival, caryatids represent the way women have traditionally carried large burdens on their heads.

Head stop

Human heads, both male and female, were commonly used as decoration during the Romanesque and Gothic periods. They served to decorate corbels and brackets and as punctuation marks, known as head stops, on architectural moldings such as those over windows and arches. Animal faces can be treated in the same way.

Cupid

Winged boy-child figures, usually holding a bow, are called cupids after the god of love, and can be used on their own or with garlands and other ornament. *Putti* (archaic Italian for "little boys") are similar, but have no wings, while a winged baby head is known as a cherub.

Herm

This half-human, half-pilaster figure is called a herm (from the Greek god Hermes) and is a frequent feature in Renaissance decoration, especially in northern Europe. In Antiquity, herms had prominent male genitalia, but these were omitted in later years, when the form became a common type of grotesque.

Atlas

A male figure who strains, with his face and body contorted, to support a building pressing down upon him is known as an Atlas (plural Atlantes), after the strongman of Greek myth. His appearance is somewhat comical. These Atlantes strain to support the door surround of a 19th-century German apartment building.

Animal Form

Animal forms can be used decoratively in a variety of different ways. As with human forms, parts of a building can take on animal form, and interact visually with the rest of the building. Animals can also be used on their own as decorative motifs, or combined with other motifs such as foliage, flowers, or humans. Grotesque, or stylized, animal forms are the most common, and are particularly characteristic of the Romanesque, Gothic, and Renaissance periods, but more lifelike forms were also used. Naturalistic animals were especially characteristic of the Classical and neoclassical periods, when even fanciful creatures like sphinxes were depicted as if alive.

Bucrania

Bucrania (Latin for "ox skulls") were commonly used during the Classical period, and again from the Renaissance onward, to decorate friezes, usually in conjunction with a floral garland. They are probably a reminder of the oxen that were sacrificed in ancient Greek and Roman religious rituals.

Beak head

Designers have always been amused by the way architectural forms seem to take on the characteristics of animals or people. Here, a Romanesque molding is being "bitten" by a stylized bird known as a beak head. Most beak heads are birdlike, but other animal and humanoid forms are also known.

Grotesque

Stylized and bizarre human or animal figures, known as grotesques, were a particular decorative feature of Gothic, Romanesque, and (as here) Renaissance decorative schemes, although they are also found in other periods. They were often used in multiples, especially as addorsed or affronted pairs, and combined with foliage.

Sphinx

The sphinx, a mythical beast that is half-human, half-lion, was a popular figure in ancient Greek and Egyptian mythology. It often guards entrances, but can also be used simply as a decorative motif. Other fantastic creatures include the harpy (half-woman, half-bird) and the centaur (half-man, half-horse).

Claw feet

Animal feet, paws, or claws were used to ornament the bases of columns as well as the legs of furniture, especially during the 18th century. These claws emerge from the base of a column, giving rein to the conceit that the structural element is actually a living thing.

Foliage

Leaves, stems, and other foliage are universally popular decorative motifs, lending themselves to a wide range of possible uses. Foliage can be extremely naturalistic and lifelike, or it can be highly stylized, taking only the essence of the leaf and reducing it to its bare essentials. It can adorn capitals, and many of the key capital forms, such as the Corinthian capital, are based on foliage designs. Trails and swirls of foliage can be used to cover large surfaces with an overall pattern, but single-leaf forms can also be used as architectural accents at key points on a building.

Acanthus leaf
The large, jagged leaf of the *Acanthus spinosus* plant has long been an inspiration to architectural designers. In particular, it appears, in a relatively naturalistic form on Corinthian capitals, such as this one from the Temple of Zeus, Athens; however, it was also the origin of later, more stylized Gothic foliage capitals.

Crocket

A swirl of stylized foliage projecting from the edge of a Gothic architectural element such as a capital, gable, or canopy is called a crocket. Crockets are commonly carved like partly unfurled leaves. Here, crockets are combined with ball-flowers to create a richer decorative effect.

Naturalistic foliage

Both stylized and naturalistic (realistic) foliage are common in architectural ornamentation. Naturalistic foliage is characteristic of the Gothic style, when masons relished the chance to create lifelike flowers, leaves, and fruit out of solid stone. These French capitals from Reims have natural oak leaves and blackberries.

Foliage trail

Intertwined foliage is a practical way of covering a large area with a relatively small amount of ornament, and variations on the theme appear in most periods of architectural history, on both rounded and flat surfaces. The example here comes from an early Renaissance pilaster.

Arabesque

Graceful scrolling designs of stylized foliage are called arabesques, and were often used as part of an overall pattern on walls. The name implies an Arabic origin but the more naturalistic designs popular in the baroque and rococo periods have relatively little to do with the more geometric designs that were favored in Islamic architecture.

Floral

Flowers of all sorts have been a popular decorative motif in all periods of architectural history, and appear both as themselves in very lifelike representations and in more stylized forms that can become almost geometric. Floral motifs are particularly characteristic of Classical (especially Greek) architecture, the Middle Ages, the baroque, and the 19th century, but there is no period in which floral motifs have not been used. As in life, flowers lend themselves to being combined with other motifs, such as foliage and fruit, to create garlands and swags, and they also suit repeating patterns, both naturalistic and geometric.

Anthemion

The anthemion is a stylized flower, based on honeysuckle, that first appeared in ancient Greek architecture and was much used later, especially in the neoclassical period. Other similar stylized flowers include the palmette, based on palm fronds, which is often used in conjunction with the anthemion, as seen here.

Rosette

The rosette, or stylized rose flower, is one of the most common motifs in architectural decoration throughout the ages, largely because the simple design of overlapping petals is so easy to create. Rosettes can be used on their own, like decorative punctuation marks, or they can form part of a larger design.

Ball-flower

One of the most characteristic aspects of English 14th-century Decorated Gothic architecture is the ball-flower, a round ball like a stylized bud with three small petals. Ball-flowers are normally used in rows to adorn the edges of doorways, arches, windows, and spires, giving an allover pattern.

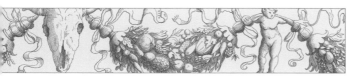

Garland

Flowers, fruit, and foliage often appear mixed together in architectural ornament. One way of doing this is to create a garland or swag, also known as a festoon, of the sort that might be made from real greenery. Garlands are frequently carved in high relief to make them more realistic-looking.

Fleur-de-lys

The fleur-de-lys is a stylized lily flower with two drooping side sections. The emblem of the French monarchy, it was widely used as a decorative motif, as here, where floor tiles are shaped into a repeating fleur-de-lys pattern. Fleur-de-lys were also a symbol of purity associated with the Virgin Mary.

Geometric

Geometric shapes of all kinds—from lines to squares, circles and crosses, and all manner of shapes in between—are a staple of ornamental design. Geometric shapes are particularly versatile because they can be scaled up or down, used in multiples to create more complex patterns, and extended infinitely to cover large areas and long distances. Such patterns have been used in all periods of architectural design, and no one period has a monopoly on them, but particular shapes are more associated with some periods than others, like the characteristic chevron of the Romanesque period, or the Classical meander.

Chevron

The chevron, or zigzag, is particularly suited for use on curved shapes such as arches, windows, and doors, because the pointed shape can be made wider or narrower to suit the curvature. Commonly associated with the Romanesque period, as here at Devizes in England, it was also popular during the Art Deco period.

Meander

Meander patterns are created from intersecting lines that turn and turn back at right angles, crossing each other as they do so. Also known as Greek key patterns, meander patterns were commonly used during ancient Greece and were also a very important part of late 18th-century neoclassical ornamental design.

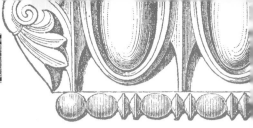

Egg-and-dart

This molding is called egg-and-dart for its resemblance to a row of eggs with their tops cut off, interspersed with darts or arrows. Here it is combined with a row of pearl beading to create a more elaborate effect. Egg-and-dart was widely used in both the Classical and Classical Revival periods for cornices and other molding bands.

Diaper pattern

Used in sets or multiples, simple X or cross shapes can form interesting and complex overall patterns, usually known as diaper, after the woven pattern used in some textiles. Diaper patterns can be carved, made of applied tiles, or created using darker and lighter bricks.

Guilloche

A pattern of interlaced circles is called guilloche. Like the meander patterns that it resembles, guilloche was used to adorn friezes and cornices, and is frequently employed to give a rich effect to cornices and ceiling moldings.

Architecture as Ornament

Architectural elements can be decorative as well as functional, and in many cases their function is primarily to provide our eyes with reassurance. Finials finish off another shape, and various types of brackets and corbels seem to support projecting elements, even though the actual structural stability is usually provided in other ways. Architectural details can also be used in purely decorative ways. Gables and tracery were commonly used in this way during the Gothic period, and pediments placed over windows and doors are symbolic representations of the gable ends of buildings. This section takes a look at a few of these decorative architectural elements.

Micro-architecture

The decoration around the base of this spire uses miniature architectural details, such as gables and niches, to create the appearance of a series of decorative miniaturized buildings. Known as micro-architecture, this was a popular decorative motif in 14th-century Gothic architecture, especially in England.

String course

A thin horizontal band placed between stories, or at another significant junction in the facade design, is called a string course. String courses were commonly used in the Romanesque and Gothic periods, and similar effects are created on later brick buildings with bands of rendered or textured brick.

Pediment

A pediment is a decorative gable that is enclosed on all three sides with a cornice molding. Pediments can be triangular, as here, or curved. This example has a broken apex with an urn finial at the center, but pediments can also have a broken base (split lower section).

Console

A console is an ornamental bracket with a scrolling reverse S-shape. It was popular in the Classical period, and in all the Classical Revival periods, for supporting projecting elements such as balconies (as in this rococo example), mantels, and cornices over doors and windows.

Canopy

A canopy is a projecting hood that is placed over another element such as a statue or, as here, a door. This shell-shaped canopy on an early American house in Connecticut has been formed from a curved pediment. Canopies were also widely used in Gothic architecture.

Molding

A molding is a continuous band, often three-dimensional, that is used to enhance an opening or decorate another architectural element, such as a capital, base, or cornice, and it was used in all periods. Moldings can take the form of shapes including rolls (often called a torus molding), hollows, and angles (such as the 45° chamfer). Almost any kind of pattern can be used to decorate a molding, but continuous patterns and repeating designs like egg-and-dart are particularly common because they can be adapted to any length. These repeating designs also come in different sizes, and some, such as modillions, can be quite large.

Modillion
This scrolling bracket placed with its long side against a horizontal surface above is called a modillion. Modillions, which are like console brackets turned horizontal, are used on the undersides of cornices. They were particularly popular as ornaments in the neoclassical period and are sometimes alternated with hollowed-out coffering panels.

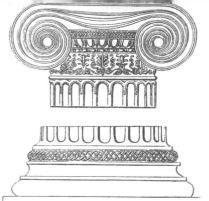

Scotia and torus

This Ionic base shows how moldings—including curves, hollows, and applied detailing—enhance an architectural element with light and shadow. The basic form of the base is tapering, but this is broken up by the hollow (or scotia) and the roll (torus). The upper torus molding has applied interlace patterns.

Chamfer

Angles can be used to soften architectural elements such as arches. Chamfers—bevel cuts across the edge of an otherwise square molding—were especially common in the Romanesque and Gothic periods, but can be found in all periods. Chamfers can be used in isolation or in combination with other moldings.

Bead-and-reel

This molding is called a bead-and-reel and looks like a string of beads. In Classical Greek architecture it was associated with the Ionic Order, but it was widely used in both the Roman period and in later periods, including the neoclassical. Variants also appear in Romanesque architecture.

Egg-and-dart

It is easy to see how this molding received its name, because it looks just like a row of rounded eggs separated by slender arrows or darts. Depending on the shape of the darts, it is sometimes also called egg-and-tongue or egg-and-anchor, and was an important element of Classical architecture and its derivatives.

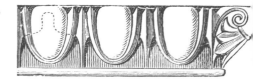

Decorative Object

Depictions of inanimate objects are often used as ornaments, and among the most popular are weapons—such as spears and bows and arrows—vases, urns, and pyramidal obelisks. Stylized depictions of objects, such as strapwork, which represents decorative leather straps, are also popular. The use of such objects, either on their own or in conjunction with foliage and other motifs, was particularly popular during the Renaissance, baroque, and neoclassical periods, when they were seen as direct references back to the Greek and Roman periods. Many objects also had allegorical or symbolic meanings that could be understood by a knowledgeable observer: urns, for instance, were evocative of death.

Cartouche

A carved wall plaque with a scrolling frame is known as a cartouche. Cartouches sometimes, but not always, contain inscriptions, figures, or scenes. They were particularly popular in baroque and rococo decoration, and were often surrounded by ribbons, banners, or trailing foliage to create an overall decorative effect.

Armorial display

Shields, crests, and other heraldic devices were extremely popular as architectural ornaments in the Middle Ages and the Renaissance. On the 17th-century gateway of Heriot's Hospital in Edinburgh, Scotland, the patron's armorial shield, with its helmet above and motto below, forms the centerpiece of an elaborate display.

Strapwork

Strapwork, so called for its resemblance to leather straps, was a popular form of decoration in northern European architecture, especially that of England and the Low Countries. Strapwork could be applied to a surface or used, as here, as a freestanding cresting, providing a play of light and shadow.

Obelisk

Tall, rectilinear shafts that taper toward the top like elongated pyramids, as on the gable of the Town Hall in Antwerp, Belgium (1561–65), are called obelisks. They were a key decorative motif in the architecture of the northern European Renaissance and were often used, as here, on gables.

Urn

An urn is a tall, curving pot with a lid. It is set on a tapering base, like this one from a design by the neoclassical architect Robert Adam. Derived from vessels used by the Romans in funeral ceremonies, urns symbolized death. A vase is similar, but has no cover.

Glossary

ACANTHUS a type of plant with deeply divided leaves.

AISLE the part of a building divided off by an arcade.

ALL'ANTICA based on antique models.

ALTAR a block or stand where offerings are made to a deity.

AMBULATORY an aisle enclosing a church choir.

ANTEFIX one of the vertical blocks used along the edge of a roof in the Classical period.

ANTHEMION stylized honeysuckle leaf.

ANTIQUITY the ancient Greek and Roman periods.

APEX the pointed top of a gable or pediment.

APPLIED made separately and added later.

APSE the curved east end of a church.

ARABESQUES scrolling foliage designs.

ARCADE a row of arches.

ARCH a curved opening.

ARCHITRAVE the lowest component of a Classical entablature; also the frame around an opening.

ASHLAR stone masonry of regular blocks.

ASTRAGAL a half-round molding.

ATLAS (PL. ATLANTES) a support in the form of a male figure.

ATRIUM an open-roofed entrance hall or central court.

ATTACHED *see* Engaged.

BALCONY a projecting gallery or walkway.

BALUSTER a vertical shaft supporting a rail.

BARGEBOARD a decorative board covering the angled sides of a roof gable.

BAROQUE the extravagant European architectural style of the 17th and 18th centuries.

BASE the lower part of a column.

BASILICA a Roman and Christian building type with an aisled nave.

BATTLEMENT a parapet with alternating high and low sections; also called crenellation.

BAY the vertical division of a building, often by windows or arches.

BCE before the current, Common, or Christian era (period).

BEAM a horizontal structural support.

BEAUX-ARTS an elaborate late 19th- and early 20th-century architectural style.

BELLCOTE a small gable holding bells.

BELL TOWER a tower for bells.

BIFORATE WINDOW a window with two openings often with a roundel above; also called a Venetian arch.

BLIND (of an arch or tracery pattern) placed against a wall without an actual opening behind it.

BLIND ARCADE a blank arcade, without openings.

BOND a pattern of laying bricks.

BOSS a central stone, locking together vault ribs.

BOW WINDOW a curved bay window.

BRACE a diagonal support linking a series of uprights.

BUCRANIA ox-skulls used as ornament, usually with garlands.

BUST the head and shoulders of a human figure.

BUTTERY a room in a medieval house for storing wet foods.

BUTTRESS a mass of masonry built against a wall to reinforce it.

CAISSON a sealed, watertight concrete structure used as a foundation in wet conditions.

CAME a lead strip holding stained glass.

CANOPY a projecting ornamental hood.

CANTED angled.

CANTILEVER an overhanging projection with no support on its outside edge.

CAPITAL the top of a column.

CARTOUCHE an ornamental frame, usually oval or round.

CARYATID a support in the form of a draped female figure.

CASEMENT WINDOW a window with hinged panes.

CE in the current, Common, or Christian era (period).

CELLA the enclosed inner sacred area of a Classical temple.

CEMENT a lime-based paste that binds together and sets hard; it is used in mortar, concrete, and as render.

CHAMFER a beveled edge.

CHAPEL a subsection of a church with its own altar, or a small church.

CHEVRON a V-shape or zigzag.

CHOIR the part of a church reserved for the singers.

CLADDING an exterior covering.

CLAPBOARD a type of wooden siding.

CLASSICAL pertaining to the ancient Greek and Roman periods.

CLERESTORY a row of high-level windows.

CLOSERS short bricks or stones around an opening.

COFFERING a pattern of sunken panels.

COLONETTE a small column.

COLONNADE a row of columns.

COLUMN a freestanding shaft, often supporting an arch or entablature.

CONCRETE a mixture of cement and aggregate (sand and stones) that dries very hard; it is used as a building material.

CONOIDS cone-shaped structures that form the fans of a fan vault.

CONSOLE a bracket support with an inward-curving scroll at the top and an outward-curving scroll at the bottom.

CORBEL a projecting block or capital supporting an arch or shaft above.

CORINTHIAN one of the five Classical Orders.

CORNICE a horizontal projecting molding, especially the topmost component of an entablature.

COTTAGE ORNÉ an "ornamental cottage" in a fanciful rural style, often intended to form part of a Picturesque landscape.

CRENELLATION *see* Battlement.

CRESTING an ornamental feature on top of a horizontal element.

CROCKET a projecting stylized foliage knob.

CROSSING the area in a church where nave, transepts, and choir intersect.

CRUCIFORM cross-shaped.

CUPOLA a small decorative form of dome.

CURTAIN WALL a thin, nonstructural wall in front of a structural frame.

CUSP a decorative point within an arch.

CYCLOPEAN MASONRY very large masonry.

DECORATED a style of English Gothic architecture.

DENTIL MOLDING a row of small square blocks.

DIAPER a pattern of repeated squares or lozenges.

DIOCLETIAN WINDOW a half-round opening with three subsections.

DORIC one of the five Classical Orders.

DORMER a window projecting from a roof.

DOUBLE-HUNG WINDOW a sash window with two sliding sections.

DOVECOTE a building for raising doves or pigeons for food.

DRIP MOLDING *see* Hood molding.

DRY STONE WALLING masonry made without mortar.

Glossary

EARED (of an architrave) with projections at the upper corners.

EAVES the part of a roof that projects beyond the wall.

EGG-AND-DART a type of molding resembling egg shapes alternating with dart shapes.

ELEVATION any of the vertical faces of a building, inside or out.

EMBRASURE the sides of a window opening.

EN DÉLIT detached (referring to a Gothic stone shaft).

ENFILADE a series of rooms leading off each other with the doors aligned.

ENGAGED (of a column) attached to the wall.

ENTABLATURE the whole of the horizontal structure above the capitals in a Classical Order.

EXEDRA(E) large niche(s).

FACADE the front exterior face of a building.

FACET one face of a geometric shape.

FANLIGHT a semicircular window over a door.

FEDERAL STYLE American neoclassical architecture of *c*.1776–*c*.1830.

FESTOON a curved foliage and fruit garland tied with ribbons.

FIELDED PANEL a square or rectangular panel with a raised central section.

FINIAL the decorative knob on top of a gable, post, or other upright.

FLAMBOYANT a late medieval style of Gothic architecture characterized by flowing motifs.

FLÈCHE a small spire, usually of lead-covered timber.

FLUE the pipe inside a chimney to conduct smoke outward.

FLUTING parallel concave channels on a column or surface.

FLYING BUTTRESS a freestanding arched buttress.

FRAMING a structural skeleton in wood or metal.

FRIEZE a decorative horizontal band, especially the central component of an entablature.

FRENCH DOORS OR WINDOWS full-length casement windows opening like doors onto a balcony or terrace.

FRESCO a painting with pigment applied directly into wet plaster.

GABLE the pointed end wall of a roof.

GALLERY an internal passage, usually open on one side.

GARGOYLE a grotesque water spout.

GARLAND a band of flowers and foliage; *see also* Festoon.

GEORGIAN English architectural style of *c*.1714–1830.

GIANT ORDER an arch encompassing two or more stories.

GLAZED made of glass; glossy.

GLAZING BAR *see* Muntin.

GOTHIC European architectural style of *c*.1150–*c*.1500.

GOTHIC REVIVAL a late 18th- and 19th-century Gothic-inspired style.

GREEK the style current in ancient Greece from the 7th to 2nd centuries BCE.

GREEK REVIVAL a late 18th- and early 19th-century style drawing on ancient Greek examples.

GROIN VAULT an intersecting barrel vault without ribs.

GROTESQUE fantastic or mythical; especially refers to figures combining human, animal, and foliage forms.

GUILLOCHE a decorative pattern of interlaced circles.

HALF-TIMBERED having exposed timber framing.

HALL an entranceway; also the main room of a medieval house.

HAMMERBEAM a short roof timber cantilevered out to carry an upright.

HEAD STOP the end of a molding that is carved with a human face.

HEARTH a fireproof floor area for making a fire.

HERALDIC using, or pertaining to, heraldry.

HERALDRY the system of coats of arms and symbolic badges.

HIPPED ROOF a roof that is pitched at the ends as well as the sides.

HISTORIATED depicting a narrative.

HOOD MOLDING a three-sided molding over a window or door; also called drip molding.

IMBREX (PL. *IMBRICES*) a curved tile used to cover joints between *tegulae*.

INFILL material used to fill spaces between the components of a framework.

IONIC one of the five Classical Orders.

JAMB the vertical part of a door or window opening.

JETTY an overhanging upper story.

JOIST a horizontal timber supporting a floor or ceiling.

KEEP the main tower of a castle.

KEYSTONE the central block locking together an arch.

LANCET a tall, narrow, pointed, early Gothic window.

LANTERN a turret or tower on top of a roof or dome to let in light.

LESENE a decorative stonework strip.

LIERNE a purely decorative vaulting rib running between two other ribs.

LIGHT the vertical section of a window.

LINTEL the beam over an opening, supported on jambs or columns.

LOGGIA a gallery with an open colonnade along one or more sides.

LOUVER a small structure or opening for ventilation.

LOZENGE a diamond shape.

LUCARNE a small Gothic dormer window.

LUNETTE a half-round window.

MACHICOLATION an opening that enabled missiles to be dropped from a parapet onto an enemy.

MANTEL a lintel or shelf above a fireplace.

MANTELPIECE the decorative structure around a fireplace.

MASK decorative human or animal face.

MASON someone who builds in stone or brick.

MASONRY stone or brick construction.

MEANDER a snaking pattern of straight lines joined at angles.

MEDIEVAL the period in European history, *c.*1000–*c.*1550 CE.

METOPE a plain or decorated slab on a Doric frieze; it alternates with triglyphs.

MICRO-ARCHITECTURE miniature architectural motifs, such as arches and gables, used decoratively.

MINARET a tower associated with a mosque, for calling the faithful to prayer.

MODERNIST the architectural style current from *c.*1920 till the late 20th century.

MODILLION a horizontal scroll bracket below a cornice.

MOLDING a strip with a shaped or decorated surface.

MORTAR a paste made of lime or cement, used in between blocks or bricks.

MORTISE a hole or slot for a tenon, which is used to join wood pieces.

MOSAIC a picture made of tiny colored tiles.

MOTIF a decorative element, usually repeated.

MOUCHETTE a teardrop shape used in Gothic tracery.

MULLION a vertical element dividing a window into sections.

Glossary

MUNTIN a small vertical or horizontal wooden bar holding the panes in a sash window; also called a glazing bar.

NAOS see *Cella*.

NARTHEX the area in an early Christian church where new converts stood.

NATURALISTIC lifelike.

NAVE the area of a church reserved for lay people.

NEOCLASSICAL an architectural style based on Classical precedents, which was fashionable in the 18th and early 19th centuries.

NEWEL the central post of a spiral stair, or the endpost of a straight stair.

NICHE an ornamental recess, often curved at the back and top.

NORMAN see Romanesque.

OBELISK a tall, four-sided tapering form.

OCULUS a round window.

OEIL-DE-BOEUF a round or oval window.

OGEE a shallow reverse-curve or S-curve.

OPISTHODOMOS an enclosed porch at the back of a Greek temple.

OPUS RETICULATUM a netlike pattern of small stone tiles set in concrete.

ORDERS the five accepted styles of Classical columns and entablatures.

ORIEL a bay window starting above ground level.

PALLADIAN in the style of Andrea Palladio (1508–1580).

PALLADIAN WINDOW an opening with two straight sidelights whose entablatures support a central arched opening.

PALMETTE a stylized palm leaf.

PANELING a decorative wooden or plaster wall covering with areas defined by moldings.

PARAPET the edge of a wall projecting above roof level.

PEDESTAL the substructure below a column or supporting a statue.

PEDIMENT the gable above a Classical portico; also a gable form used decoratively.

PELMET see Valance.

PENDENTIVE a curved triangular area between a round dome and its rectangular base.

PERISTYLE a Classical colonnade around a building or courtyard.

PERPENDICULAR a 15th-century style of English Gothic architecture, characterized by paneled effects on walls and windows.

PICTURESQUE literally "like a picture," a late 18th-century aesthetic movement that stressed variety and drama.

PIER a masonry support like a column, but larger and more solid.

PILASTER a flat column form, usually attached to a wall.

PILLAR a column or pier.

PINNACLE an ornamental structure, usually pointed, on top of a buttress or other structure.

PITCH the slope of a roof.

PLAN a horizontal section or drawing showing the arrangement of spaces in a building.

PLASTER finely ground lime or gypsum paste for interior wall finishings.

PLATE GLASS large sheet glass.

PLINTH a plain projecting support at the bottom of a wall, column, or other upright.

PODIUM a platform supporting a Classical temple.

POLYCHROME multicolored.

PORCH a partially enclosed space in front of a door.

PORTAL a door.

PORTE-COCHÈRE a covered passage allowing access for vehicles, or an open porch large enough to drive under.

PORTICO a covered area with a colonnaded front.

POST a vertical timber support.

PURLIN a horizontal beam along the length of a roof.

PUTLOG HOLE a gap left in masonry to support scaffolding.

PUTTO (PL. PUTTI) naked boy figure.

QUATREFOIL a four-lobed shape.

QUEEN ANNE an eclectic 19th-century style with mixed Gothic and baroque detailing.

QUOIN large block used to strengthen angles and corners.

RAFTER a long, angled roof timber supporting the covering.

RENAISSANCE the revival of Classical forms and learning in Italy in the 15th and 16th centuries, and in the 16th and 17th centuries in northern Europe.

RENDER a paste of cement and aggregate (sand or stones) used as a waterproof wall covering; also called stucco.

RESPOND an attached half-shaft at the ends of an arcade.

REVEAL the vertical inner face of an opening.

RIB an arched molding on a vault.

RIDGE the top edge of a roof.

RISER the vertical part of a step.

ROCOCO a light and delicate 18th-century style.

ROMAN pertaining to ancient Rome, and especially the Roman Empire, 27 BCE—330 CE

ROMANESQUE the architectural style of *c.*1000–1200 CE; also known as Norman in England and Normandy.

ROTUNDA a circular room.

ROUNDEL a small circular frame or motif.

RUBBLE masonry with irregularly shaped blocks.

RUNDBOGENSTIL German for "round-arched style," a mid-19th-century revival style using motifs from different periods. Sometimes called Richardsonian Romanesque in the US after one of its practitioners, Henry Hobhouse Richardson (1838–1886).

RUSTICATION masonry cut so that the center of each block projects.

SASH WINDOW a window with vertically (or occasionally horizontally) sliding wooden frames holding the glass panes.

SCAGLIOLA a paste made of pigment, plaster, and glue.

SCOTIA a hollow molding.

SCROLL an S-shaped curve.

SEMIDOME a half-dome.

SERLIAN WINDOW a Palladian window; also known as a Venetian window.

SHAFT the cylindrical body of a column.

SHINGLE a wooden tile; also a late 19th-century American architectural variation of the Queen Anne style.

SHUTTERS wooden doors used to cover a window.

SIDING an exterior wall covering made of parallel strips of wood or other materials.

SOFFIT the underside of an architectural component, such as an arch.

SPANDREL the triangular area between an arch and its rectangular surround.

SPIRE the tall, tapering top of a church tower; also called a steeple.

SPLAY an angled surface.

SPOLIA reused materials, often with a symbolic meaning.

SPRINGER the blocks from which a vault rises.

SQUINCH the filling between a dome and the building below; less sophisticated than a pendentive.

STAINED GLASS colored glass.

STALL RISER the solid lower section of a store window.

STEEPLE *see* Spire.

Glossary

STORY a level, or floor, of a building.

STRAPWORK a decorative pattern resembling leather straps.

STRING the diagonal side of a staircase; it can be closed (solid) or open (showing the ends of the treads and risers).

STRING COURSE a raised horizontal molding that visually divides stories; also called a plat band.

STUCCO *see* Render.

STYLIZED abstract or symbolic in depiction.

STYLOBATE the upper step of the base or podium of a Classical temple.

SUBDOME a partial dome, often used to support a larger dome.

SURROUND a frame or architrave.

TAS-DE-CHARGE the point at which vault ribs begin to emerge or spring from the wall surface.

TEMPLE a religious building, especially Greek or Roman.

TENON the projection inserted into a mortise to join two pieces of wood.

TEGULA **(PL.** *TEGULAE***)** Roman roof tile, originally flat but later having small raised edges to support an *imbrex* tile over the joint.

TERRACE a row of houses joined together; a raised platform in a garden.

TIERCERON a decorative rib running between a structural rib and the central ridge rib.

TORUS a half-round or roll molding.

TOURELLE a small turret projecting from the wall above ground level.

TOWER a structure that is considerably taller than it is wide.

TRABEATED a form of construction with vertical posts and horizontal beams (lintels).

TRACERY the decorative stone bars in a Gothic window.

TRANSEPT a part of a church that projects at right angles from the nave.

TRANSOM horizontal bar across a window; also the upper part of a door frame.

TREAD the horizontal part of a step.

TREFOIL a three-lobed form.

TRIFORIUM the middle story of a Gothic cathedral.

TRIGLYPH a three-grooved panel on a Doric frieze; it alternates with metopes.

TRUMEAU a post in the center of a portal supporting the center of the tympanum.

TUDOR the period of English history from 1485 to 1603.

TUFA a type of lightweight volcanic stone.

TURRET a small tower, especially one starting above ground level.

TUSCAN one of the five Classical Orders.

TYMPANUM the area between a door lintel and an arch above.

VALANCE the fabric or wooden covering above a window; also called a pelmet.

VAULT a curved stone ceiling.

VENETIAN ARCH *see* Biforate window.

VICTORIAN pertaining to the reign of Queen Victoria, 1837–1901.

VILLA a country house or suburban house.

VOLUTE a spiral curve or scroll.

VOUSSOIR a wedge-shaped block in an arch.

WEATHERBOARDING a type of wooden siding.

WEATHERVANE a pivoting roof ornament to show wind direction.

WEBBING the surfaces between the ribs of a vault.

WING the side part of a building.

Index

Index

Index

AUTHOR ACKNOWLEDGMENTS

I am very grateful to Dominique Page and the team at Ivy Press for doing such a good job in often trying circumstances. This book could not have been written without James Stevens Curl's *Oxford Dictionary of Architecture*, so many thanks to him for that labor of love and also to the numerous other authors I consulted along the way. In particular, Albert Rosengarten, Russell Sturgis, E. E. Viollet-le-Duc, J. H. Parker, and James Fergusson not only illustrated many of the buildings and other architectural items included in this book but taught me a great deal along the way. And finally, my biggest debts are to my wonderfully supportive husband Matthew and to Felicity, who helped in her own unique feline way.

PUBLISHER ACKNOWLEDGMENTS

Ivy Press would like to thank Sears Holdings Archives for kindly giving permission for the use of their images.